PERFECT PHRASES™

for

CREATIVITY

AND

INNOVATION

PERFECT PHRASES™

for

CREATIVITY

AND

INNOVATION

**Hundreds of ready-to-use phrases for
breakthrough thinking, inventive problem solving,
and team collaboration**

Karen Eriksen

New York   Chicago   San Francisco   Lisbon   London   Madrid   Mexico City
Milan   New Delhi   San Juan   Seoul   Singapore   Sydney   Toronto

1 2 3 4 5 6 7 8 9 0   QFR/QFR   1 8 7 6 5 4 3 2

ISBN   978-0-07-178294-4
MHID   0-07-178294-X

e-ISBN   978-0-07-178295-1
e-MHID   0-07-178295-8

This publication is designed to provide accurate and authoritative informa-tion in regard to the subject matter covered. It is sold with the understand-ing that neither the author nor the publisher is engaged in rendering legal, accounting, securities trading, or other professional service. If legal advice or other expert assistance is required, the services of a competent professional person should be sought.
    —*From a Declaration of Principles Jointly Adopted by a Committee of the American Bar Association and a Committee of Publishers and Associations*

McGraw-Hill books are available at special quantity discounts to use as pre-miums and sales promotions or for use in corporate training programs. To contact a representative, please e-mail us at bulksales@mcgraw-hill.com.

This book is printed on acid-free paper.

To Kerry Johnson and Jim Cox of Hemsley Fraser, who believed in me, encouraged me, and gave me confidence in a new career as a trainer.

To Anne Bruce, who mentored the development of this book and is ever the ultrapositive and reinforcing guide.

To my daughter, the actor, who focuses me on what really matters and, in being creative herself, reminds me of the joy of creativity.

Contents

Introduction

Today, people and businesses alike are discovering change all around them—some of it good and some not so good, but all of it inevitable and unavoidable. As a result, companies and organizations can no longer succeed without ongoing innovation, without regularly reinventing themselves, and without transformational change that moves beyond incremental, step-by-step problem solving. Problem solving—the day-to-day, rational-brain process of systematic thinking, review, and strategic planning, in fairly predictable steps along a well-defined dimension—*is* still necessary. But problem solving is simply not sufficient for success in today's business environment. Innovation, in contrast, moves organizations and their people "out of the box"; it moves beyond incremental rational thinking to involve the whole brain, the whole person. As Frans Johansson, author of *The Medici Effect*, says, the necessary innovation is surprising and fascinating, takes leaps in new directions that last for years or decades, opens up new fields, generates followers, creates leaders, and affects the world in unprecedented ways. And as Teresa Amabile of Harvard Business School indicates, "All innovation begins with creative ideas."

So, how do we get creative? How do we bring creativity into the workplace? Can we be intentionally creative, or does creativity just happen? Do we have to be born creative? How do we define creativity? Christopher Peterson and Martin Seligman, in their book *Character Strengths and Virtues*, challenge us to think about creativity in terms of three factors:

■ How creative a product is
■ What underlies the creative process
■ Characteristics of creative people

They include the following in their definitions of creativity:

■ Activities in which people find a sense of purpose and joy while bringing happiness and meaning to others
■ The ability to generate ideas or behaviors that are novel, surprising, or unusual
■ Generating original ideas or behaviors that make a contribution to someone's life by being workable or useful

They distinguish between the creativity of the true masters and the ingenuity necessary to generate creative solutions to various day-to-day problems that face us at home or at work. The creativity involved in ingenuity is accessible to everyone. According to Daniel Goleman, Paul Kaufman, and Michael Ray, authors of *The Creative Spirit,* such ingenuity is the way "each of us displays flair and imagination in our own lives," going beyond the routine and conventional, and giving each of us a great deal of pleasure. Sidney Parnes agrees: "Every human being has the potential to be creative, if given the opportunity and the right environment." Creativity "is a skill that can be strengthened with coaching and practice." Parnes's mental model for creativity uses *divergent* thinking to expand the available options and *convergent* thinking to focus on the preferred, innovative choice.

Creativity can belong to everyone because most creativity is a matter of borrowing from others and combining their ideas in new ways. As David Murray points out in *Borrowing Brilliance,* before the fourteenth century, creativity and innovation were understood to be collaborative efforts in which one idea was copied from another and evolved through incremental enhancements. The concept of plagiarism didn't exist. Copying and creating were rooted in the same thing. The person who copied had an obligation to improve the copy; that was it. Creators and artists didn't even sign their work until the beginning of the sixteenth century. Through the mid-1800s, the key to value in products was availability and price, not originality. It wasn't until much later that we began to think in terms of originality and intellectual property.

So Murray's perspective, and that of other creativity experts, is that all of us can access our inherent creativity by systematically constructing new ideas out of existing ideas. Instead of a waiting game, he says, creativity is an intentional exploration game—"the search for an idea that already exists, not the act of waiting for one to pop into your head." He urges us to stand on the shoulders of giants in order to see further, claiming that ideas naturally evolve over time, and that there is a fine line between theft and originality. "Ideas are constructed out of other ideas," he says. "There are no truly original thoughts. We can't make something out of nothing. We have to make it out of something else." And so, we need to invest intentionally in creativity-inspiring processes, not merely in hiring creative people.

What is clear is that, as Tom Peters says, "Innovation must become every firm's 'Job One.'" It can't be outsourced. It has to become part of the DNA of every organization. Vincent Cassandro and Dean Simonton, who write about creativity and genius, agree: "At the group level, the importance of creativity to the growth, health, and well-being of society cannot be understated. . . . The history of creative products and ideas can be thought of as an extension from past to future generations—a cross-generational interconnectedness fostered by the generative possibilities of the human mind."

And so, this book can help leaders, managers, and supervisors to get the best out of themselves and their teams, both in day-to-day interactions and in intentional creativity meetings. It offers lists of perfect phrases and activities to bring the best of what we know about creativity into everyone's workplaces.

Perfect Phrases for Creativity and Innovation brings creativity and innovation into the realm of possibility for managers and leaders at all levels—for entry-level supervisors, for seasoned supervisors, and for employees and teams who want to kick-start creative thinking in their groups and take innovative solution finding up a notch. It offers easy-to-implement phrases and activities for initiating creative thinking that will then become go-to, must-have tips, tools, and techniques for a more effective, solution-driven, exciting, and thought-provoking work environment.

Creativity and innovation begin with you! Creative products require a creative process. Creative employees require creative leaders who intentionally lead their people toward innovative and transformative change. And so, after we examine the "essentials" underlying creativity in this introduction, Chapter 1 focuses on jump-starting our own creativity. Chapter 2 offers perfect phrases for motivating groups and teams to be highly creative. Chapter 3 outlines the necessary steps to complete creativity initiatives, including problem definition, evaluation, and action and communication planning. Chapter 4 offers perfect phrases for creativity-inducing activities that trigger whole-brain, divergent thinking. Chapter 5 aims toward creating work environments that stimulate creativity. Chapter 6 offers a vision of "extreme" options, such as using the creative arts and team challenges to trigger innovation. Chapter 7 challenges creative people and organizations to celebrate success. And Chapter 8 offers examples of companies that have succeeded at creativity. Welcome to the process! This is your entry into a new adventure!

The Elements of Creativity

What makes a person or a company creative? How do organizations or individuals access and maximize their creative potential? What are the most successful innovators and companies doing to stay on the cutting edge, to keep producing exciting new products, and to stay in the public eye as a result of their creations? A great deal of research has sought to answer these questions. Researchers and creativity experts seem to agree that the creativity of individuals and groups can be enhanced by:

- Believing that *many answers exist*, that we will find them, and that they are necessary to success
- Creating *environments* that are *supportive* of creativity
- Finding our *calling* or being in the *flow*
- *Valuing ourselves*
- Accessing the power of the *group* or *community*
- Using our *whole brain*
- Increasing *divergent* thinking
- Bringing our *whole selves*, including our inner child, to the creativity table
- Staying *open* to many different people, experiences, and sources of information
- Intentionally and regularly engaging in and trusting in the *process* of creativity

These principles are spelled out here, and the remainder of the book's chapters offer perfect phrases and activities for actualizing these principles.

Answers Exist

Creatively and energetically pursuing answers to business or organizational problems requires the belief that:

- Answers exist.
- They are out there somewhere.
- There are many possible answers, not just one or two good ones, that can turn an industry around and have the potential for real moneymaking.
- We will find these creative answers.
- In fact, anyone can find them—it doesn't take a genius.
- Creative ideas are accessible to anyone who engages in creativity-inducing processes.
- We can find inspiration in knowing that there are many answers out there.
- Creativity is necessary for success in business and other organizations.

Supportive Environment

Creativity and innovation require a supportive environment; judgment is tremendously harmful to the creative process. Leaders who recognize the value of creativity at all levels and all phases of business, including creating new and improved versions of products, intentionally create a culture that encourages creativity, a culture that:

- Supports creative people and teams
- Allocates resources to creative processes
- Recognizes the value of reducing hierarchy
- Aims to create vast volumes of ideas
- Understands that often many failures precede great success
- Rewards quantities of ideas and outputs
- Allocates resources for many trials
- Reduces surveillance, evaluation, extrinsic rewards, competition, overcontrol, and pressure (especially time pressure) because they are harmful to the creative impulse

Flow or Calling

Historically, creativity was associated with "the divine," rather than "the human." As Christopher Peterson and Martin Seligman indicate, "Outstanding creativity was the gift of the gods or spirits, not a human act." But whatever our spiritual leanings, it is clear that most creative people consider the creative process to involve:

- A spiritual experience
- A process of being "in the flow" of life and paying close attention
- Tasks that seem to come from some essential place within
- A sense of surrendering to an "inner vision"
- The very purpose of human existence
- Operating from a sense of a "calling," or our center, or of doing what we love or what gives us joy
- Finding ourselves completely absorbed by the work and by the sheer joy of the task
- Letting go, which in turn allows what already exists to be manifested
- Tuning in and dropping into an already existing underground well of ideas
- Becoming more the conduit than the creator of what they express
- Something more like eavesdropping and less like inventing a nuclear bomb
- Getting out of the way and letting "it" work through you
- Getting acquainted with your own essential qualities and expressing them in your daily activities
- Living every moment from your Essence
- Taking a leap of faith

As Julia Cameron says in *The Artist's Way*, "Beyond the reach of the Censor's babble we find our own quiet center, the place where we hear the still, small voice that is at once our creator's and our own."

Valuing Ourselves

Creativity and innovation require exposing ourselves to risk, and facing risks takes:

- Courage, self-confidence, and total commitment
- Refusing to let failure have the last word
- A spirit of asking, "Why not?"
- Sheer audacity and bold tenacity
- Belief in ourselves and in our ideas, "no holds barred"
- Being fully committed to taking action
- A clear sense of identity and hope
- Persistently pursuing expertise in a particular domain
- A certain level of self-actualization
- Reaching for desires and dreams
- Self-care and recovery from the past voices of doubt
- Becoming the subject in our lives, the one who initiates and takes action, rather than the object of everyone else's activities and desires—merely a reactor
- The ability to visualize ourselves creating and succeeding, surmounting any obstacles, and recovering from the inevitable failures
- Challenging the voices of judgment that inhibit creativity
- Looking inside and fanning the flames of creativity that lie within ourselves
- Knowing and using our whole self

The Community and Small Groups

In addition to needing a supportive workplace environment and a strong sense of self to support the creative process, creativity requires harnessing the power of the group. In most cases, creativity:

- Is a community affair
- Results from interactions that we have with others
- Involves borrowing from others
- Requires an environment of supportive others who join together in a united effort
- Reaches beyond what individuals can accomplish
- Occurs in teams where the whole is more than the sum of the parts
- Emanates from a "between," a synergy, an energy in which one person builds on another's ideas
- Depends on differences among people who challenge one another:
  - ❑ To think differently
  - ❑ To become more
  - ❑ To enter into the adventure of growing and learning
  - ❑ To leave the rut of the known and to branch out into the unknown where creative ideas live
- Sometimes requires struggling together to become a creative team

Whole-Brain Thinking

Typical day-to-day workplace operations draw heavily on the left-brain activities of systematically, linearly, and logically planning, justifying, and carrying out day-to-day activities. These rational, step-by-step processes keep the "machine" functioning adequately or fix it when it breaks. However, when the real-life challenges exceed the machine's capacities, the problem-solving left brain alone will not create a new machine. Step-by-step incremental processes are simply not sufficient for success in today's business environment. Instead, creativity and innovation push organizations and their people:

- "Out of the box"
- Toward the right-brain activities of:
  - Divergence
  - Intuition
  - Analogy
  - Visualization
  - Conceiving holistic pictures
  - Synthesizing patterns and shadings
  - Considering many, many ideas

The Whole Self

In addition to needing both sides of our brain, creativity flourishes when we recognize and use the rest of our "self." Beyond thinking lie our other intelligences, without which we cannot function optimally. Creativity is a holistic process, and so, in order to access our creative potential, we need to tune in to, care for, and include in our lives our:

- Feelings
- Bodies
- Relationships
- Visual senses
- Nature
- Sounds or music

Accessing "Child"

Children are terrific at accessing their nonlinear, nonthinking selves, and as a result, they have a great deal of fun and are very playful. Our creative efforts will also benefit from:

- Fun and playfulness
- Laughter
- Moving beyond the sensible and the logical
- Considering the possible and the yet-to-be-created
- Adopting a childlike sense of:
  - ❑ Wonderment
  - ❑ Discovery
  - ❑ Exploration
  - ❑ Boundaryless anticipation

Children are constantly creating and discovering. We would do well to emulate them in our creative endeavors.

Openness

Creative people have a voracious appetite for the new and for variety. They:

- Welcome new experiences and new information
- Pursue various fields of knowledge
- Interact with many different types of people
- Program changes into their lives
- Challenge their habits in order to ward off stagnation and stay out of ruts
- Approach life as a question
- Ask "dumb" questions without expectations, assumptions, illusions, or interest in hearsay
- Are tremendously curious

- Pay close attention
- Listen carefully
- Are open to the moment
- Stay completely aware of everything around them
- Find the intersections between different fields, experiences, and people
- Are intelligent

But as Malcolm Gladwell, the author of *Blink: The Power of Thinking Without Thinking,* says, it takes an IQ of only 125 to 130 to come up with great ideas. After that, it is all about hard work and lots of practice. Genius is not necessary for creativity.

Process

And finally, creative people and teams realize that creativity and innovation:

- are a process
- a journey into the unknown
- with no prior knowledge of the bumps that one may encounter or of the destination

Staying on the road rather than jumping into the nearest restaurant requires trust that:

- The answers will come.
- There is a reward at the end of the journey.
- The adventure of the journey will lead somewhere terrific.
- Living fully into the creative process rather than rushing to a conclusion is what produces the best results.

Staying in a "not knowing" place for a period of time overchallenges some people. The journey has risks, and risks make us anxious. But as Daniel Goleman, Paul Kaufman, and Michael Ray say, "Anxiety is the handmaiden of creativity." And as Oscar Wilde once said, knowing the anxiety that is often involved in the journey toward creativity, "The anxiety is unbearable, but I only hope it lasts forever."

PERFECT PHRASES™

for

CREATIVITY

AND

INNOVATION

CHAPTER 1

Creativity Begins with Me

Assessing and Encouraging Ourselves

It would be nice if we could just say to everyone around us in our workplace or organization, "Okay, here are the elements of creativity—get started! Use them! Be creative!" But as with most things, creativity generally requires us to start with ourselves. Not only do we need to understand creativity and become creative ourselves, but we have to be able to recognize and encourage creativity in others. And if we are leaders, managers, and supervisors, we need to take responsibility for creating an environment in which creativity can flourish, an environment that is free from judgment, that provides resources for innovation, and that intentionally allocates regular time for creativity-generating activities, meetings, and retreats. So this chapter asks you to assess yourself and start the discovery processes necessary for becoming creative and for stimulating creativity around you. It offers you perfect phrases, questions, and activities related to the elements of creativity that were described in the introduction.

One caveat: not everyone has the ability to make intentional use of these elements. Intentionality requires a level of self-awareness and proactivity, and a commitment to building new strengths into our lives—all of which require reaching a certain level of developmental capacity. Did you know that our development extends in predictable stages beyond childhood? And the elements of creativity—self-confidence and the ability to manage different perspectives, to be tenacious, or to become aware of our whole selves—are all developmental accomplishments. If creativity is at the apex of human development, we have to recognize that not everyone will be able to harness what is necessary to rise to those heights. However, even those who might not *initiate* or be in charge of creative endeavors may respond well when others structure the creative process. Further, even without being initiators, they may, even on their own, connect rather unconsciously to a "source" or "well" of creativity.

In the world of adult development, we would say that the self-confidence, tenacity, and understanding of ourselves that are necessary for creativity and for answering the questions that will be posed in the perfect phrases in this book require us to know ourselves and to have the ability to make choices for our lives and to be the authors of our own lives, rather than being directed by others or defined by others' choices for us. Various writers have called these capacities "self-authoring," "postconventional knowing," or the "I am" stage of development. However, if you hadn't already attained the developmental stage required for becoming intentionally creative, or weren't already moving in that direction, you probably wouldn't have picked up this book. But since we will also be talking in this book about how to trigger creativity in others, it is important that we know what to do when we encounter people who haven't yet reached the I am or self-authoring stage. When those people are faced with the challenges of the perfect phrases in this book, they will need support to keep them from being overwhelmed or overchallenged. And support, from an adult development perspective, means that you, as a manager, leader, or supervisor, will need to:

- Give clear directions and rules for the process.
- Structure creativity events very clearly.
- Provide handouts and outlines.
- Designate certain times for creativity-enhancing discussions.
- Establish time boundaries for the process (for example, we will brainstorm for 30 minutes; we will evaluate and categorize our ideas for 30 minutes after that; and so on).
- Move on, after the "looseness" and "divergence" of innovation meetings, to structured plans for next steps, timelines, and other actions.

If you structure creativity activities in this way, you will ensure that those who are in need of support during the creative endeavor receive it without your having to directly evaluate their developmental capacities.

The following phrases offer opportunities and challenges for assessing and triggering your own and others' creativity.

Perfect Phrases to Assess Your Creativity Quotient

Do I Share the Characteristics of Creative People? Am I:

→ A master in my chosen field
→ Capable

- Clever
- Confident
- Humorous
- Individualistic
- Informal
- Insightful
- Intelligent
- Interested in many things
- Inventive
- Original
- Reflective
- Resourceful
- Self-confident
- Unconventional
- Curious
- Intrinsically motivated
- Open to new experiences and ideas
- Flexible behaviorally and cognitively
- Willing to take risks
- Bold
- Nonconformist
- Independent
- Persistent
- Motivated
- Interested in the unfamiliar, the mysterious, and the complex
- Free from fear of criticism
- A problem solver
- Unstoppable
- Brave
- Intuitive
- Trusting
- Centered

- Committed
- In the "flow"
- Following a "call"
- Playful
- Joyful
- Fun
- Courageous
- Relational
- Questioning
- Challenging
- Attentive
- Encouraging

Have I Had Leaders, Managers, Supervisors, Teachers, Parents, Mentors, or Collaborators Who:

- Were flexible.
- Supported free exploration with time and money.
- Were committed to ongoing education.
- Offered opportunities for intellectual, cultural, and aesthetic stimulation.
- Encouraged the development of independent interests.
- Challenged me to acquire considerable expertise within my chosen domain of creative activity.
- Avoided judgment.
- Recognized the value of failures.
- Avoided overcontrol.
- Left me on my own to explore.

Answers Exist—Do I Believe That:

- Answers already exist?
- There are many possible answers?
- Creative ideas are out there to discover?

→ All I have to do is search and I will find many possible solutions?

→ There are millions of ideas out there?

→ I need just one or two ideas?

→ Ideas are not hard to find?

→ The more ideas I come up with, the better?

→ If I listen carefully, I will hear many possibilities?

→ There is an eternal source of answers to tap into?

→ I can dip my net into that source and come out with many answers?

→ Solutions can be created by combining and borrowing what's already out there?

→ The creative search for answers is a way of life?

→ I can participate in that way of life?

→ I can free up my own creativity?

Flow or Calling

→ How do I access what is larger than myself?

→ How frequently do I find myself in the flow, having peak experiences, and as a result accessing unusual energy?

→ Do I see my work as a vocation or a calling—something that is very central to my life and identity?

→ What is the meaning of my life, and how does that relate to my work and to my relationships at work?

→ To what degree do I take time out for reflection or quiet, or perhaps take time to connect with what is "higher" in life?

→ Do I take the time to pray or meditate, empty myself, or focus internally so as to pay attention to my essence?

→ How often do I listen to my own center, so as to hear the still, small voice inside?

→ Do I love what I am doing? Am I experiencing great joy? Am I loving life?

→ Am I enthusiastic about what I am working on?

→ How often do I operate from my center, from my true purpose in life?

→ Do I experience an integration between my work and who I am?

→ Is my soul at work with me?

→ Am I being myself?

→ Am I living out my life's purpose?

→ Am I connected with what gives my life meaning and purpose?

→ Do I believe that there is a creative source within me? Am I tapping into that source?

→ How often do I surrender to that creative source?

→ Do I believe that creativity is oxygen for our souls?

→ Do I listen to what's at my core or to some higher power?

→ Do I believe that there is a source of abundance out there for me to tap into?

→ Do I understand how to listen to that abundance?

→ Do I listen to it frequently enough?

→ Do I believe in my calling?

→ Do I experience a sense of power when I am working on an idea—a sense of being more than I am or of connecting to something that is greater than I am?

→ How often do I get out of the way and let the creative force work through me?

→ Do I understand how to align with the creative energy of the universe?

→ How often do I have a vision for the future or for change?

→ Do I stand up for my vision even in the face of challenge?

→ How often do I listen carefully to the voice within?

→ Do I use concentration techniques like meditation and yoga to empty myself, to focus internally, to quiet my mind, to focus on my heart's leading, or to focus on my highest reality? How often do I do this?

▮ Valuing Myself

→ Do I see myself as capable and able to make a difference?
→ Do I have a sense of personal power?
→ Do I believe in myself and my ideas?
→ Am I committed to taking action?
→ Do I feel strong and able to take action?
→ Am I proactive rather than reactive in my pursuit of creativity and innovation?
→ How often do I let my anxiety and lack of confidence interfere with my creativity and innovation?
→ Am I open to growth, personally, professionally, and interpersonally, as I discover my own and others' gifts and answers?
→ Do I see myself as capable, creative, and tenacious?
→ Do I value myself enough to take care of my body by exercising, eating right, and taking enough downtime?
→ How confident am I in myself? In my creativity?
→ Do I know and accept my limitations? Do I try to overcome them?
→ Do I have the strength of commitment to endure many defeats, lack of acceptance, or naysayers?
→ How committed am I to my vision?
→ Do I have the strength of my convictions?
→ Do I know how to challenge the inevitable negative thoughts?
→ Do I believe that failure is part of success?
→ Can I get back on the horse after a failure?
→ Do I trust my creativity?
→ Do I define myself as creative or as able to be creative?

→ How accepting of myself am I?
→ Do I take care of myself emotionally and relationally?
→ Do I trust my own intuition?
→ Am I bold, tenacious, and committed to my ideas?
→ Have I let go of perfectionism, giving myself a break?
→ Do I accept my limitations or stretch beyond them?
→ Am I jealous of others' creative ideas? Or do I believe that I am just as capable of creating?
→ Do I feel strong?
→ Am I acting on my true self or betraying my true self?
→ Am I creating a safe space in which to express myself?
→ Am I actively engaged in discovering myself?
→ Do I love myself?
→ Do I believe that creativity comes from within me, that I can locate it, and that I can catch it?
→ Am I overly anxious or fearful?
→ Do I have high standards?
→ Am I an independent person?
→ Am I persistent in pursuing creative answers?
→ Do I see mistakes as opportunities to learn, rather than embarrassments?
→ Do I ensure that I have several projects going at once, rather than limiting my focus and my good feelings about myself to success on one project?
→ Can I ward off the voice of judgment?
→ Am I limited by fears?
→ Do I believe that I am smart and talented?
→ Am I dedicated and determined?
→ Do I have confidence in myself as a finder and creator of ideas?
→ Do I believe that I am a font of ideas?
→ Do I learn from my mistakes?

→ Do I pick myself up and keep going?

→ Am I a self-starter, or am I overly reliant on other people?

→ Am I an actor or a reactor?

→ Do I follow through with my intentions?

→ Do I affirm myself regularly?

→ Can I visualize myself as a success in creatively solving a problem? Do I do this regularly?

→ Do I take downtime—unstructured, unorganized time?

→ Am I persistent?

→ Do I take risks?

Communities or Small Groups

→ Have I instituted regular "creativity and innovation" meetings?

→ Am I creating and using teams regularly? Am I doing this when creative ideas are needed?

→ Have I created a team around me that I trust, filled with members who trust me, so that we can be fully truthful with one another?

→ How do I enhance the cooperativeness (rather than the competitiveness) of my team so as to enhance creativity and innovation?

→ To what degree is my team supportive, helpful, and encouraging?

→ How am I doing at being supportive, helpful, and encouraging with my team?

→ If we are running short on creative ideas, do I bring in more and different people to help us?

→ How often do I create teams to solve problems?

→ Have I brought the new hires into the creativity team? Have I initiated them into the creativity group process?

→ Have I ensured that there is enough difference in my teams—difference in professions, departments, skills, interests, cultures, passions, temperaments, and knowledge?

→ Do we have enough energy in our small group meetings?

Whole-Brain Thinking

→ To what degree am I reaching beyond my rational brain?

→ What's the ratio between how much I use my rational brain and how much I use my nonrational brain?

→ How frequently do I take a break from my rational mind?

→ Do I always have to make sense?

→ How many different ideas do I come up with before I make a decision?

→ How novel, surprising, or unusual are the ideas that I come up with?

→ How many innovative strategies has my team come up with in the past year?

→ How often am I in situations where we are dreaming up new ideas?

→ There are many ideas out there. Am I considering as many of them as I can?

→ Do I tune in to patterns and shadings?

→ Do I ensure that my creative process is freewheeling enough?

→ Do I regularly access and record my dreams?

→ Do I use visualization or drawing pictures as part of creativity meetings?

→ How successful am I in building on other people's ideas?

→ How am I doing in finding ideas to borrow and combine?

→ How many new combinations have I come up with recently?

Whole Self

→ How much of myself do I bring to the table when solving problems?

→ How often do I daydream or remember my dreams in order to access my unconscious knowledge?

→ Am I exercising my physical body as well as my mind?

→ Am I honoring my happy, sad, angry, and fearful feelings by thinking about them, talking about them, and figuring out what to do about them?

→ Am I happy with my life as I am living it now?

→ Am I happy with being me?

→ How often do I meditate, do yoga, or exercise in order to take care of myself?

→ How often do I take a walk and get out of the office?

→ How frequently do I read a new book, one that is outside of my area of expertise?

→ How frequently do I change my environment in some dramatic way?

→ How often do I go somewhere peaceful to think and to observe?

→ How frequently do I shift the senses I am using?

→ Do I ask myself frequently enough about my gut reaction, or what my intuition tells me?

Accessing "Child"

→ Do I have any fun while I am creating?

→ Do I enjoy the journey as much as I do arriving at the destination?

→ Do I take the time to stop and notice the little things?

→ Do I ever view a situation through a child's eyes?

→ Do I engage in an activity for the sheer joy of it?

→ How often do I use my senses to explore a challenge?

→ How often do I laugh?

→ Do I have fun at work more generally?

→ How often do I experience real joy when we are working on a problem?

→ Do I find myself playing during our creativity sessions?

→ Are we having any fun yet?

→ How often do I encourage my coworkers to try something totally outrageous?

→ How often do I become a child when I am facing a new problem?

→ How frequently do I joke around or tell a good joke at work?

→ How often do I find myself laughing in our creativity sessions or as we work on solving a problem?

Openness

→ When facing a challenge, to what degree do I value diversity of opinions, culture, talents, and interests?

→ How often do I discuss issues with people who are different from myself (in terms of talents, philosophy, interests, or culture)?

→ Am I staying open to the social, political, and cultural contexts that affect the team, the workplace, and our future as a company?

→ How aware am I of the ethical and values implications of the challenges we are facing and the creative choices we are considering?

→ How do I expose myself to a broad range of social ideas, minority views, and new information?

→ Do I stay open to new ideas?

→ Do I do one new, different, and nonroutine thing each day?

- → Do I regularly try to see commonplace things in a fresh way?
- → Do I listen carefully to other people?
- → How often do I try to invent new things?
- → Do I use my eyes as if tomorrow I will be blind?
- → Do I use my ears as if tomorrow I will be unable to hear?
- → Do I touch things as though I soon might not be able to feel anything?
- → Do I smell everything I can?
- → How well do I stay in the moment, staying completely aware of what's around me?
- → Do I notice exceptions and patterns?
- → How often do I pursue new knowledge? Take a course? Read a new book? Try to learn something new?
- → Have I developed a questioning attitude about the world?
- → How often do I ask questions?
- → Am I afraid to ask dumb questions?
- → Am I curious about many things?
- → Do I have a "bucket list" that I am trying to accomplish?
- → How often do I get out and meet new people?
- → Do I take every opportunity to fill my head with new information?
- → Do I travel as much as I can?
- → Do I approach the world in a way that allows me to find novel possibilities?
- → Do I turn things over in my mind, turn the world upside down, or try to view the world differently?

Process

- → Am I willing to wrestle with my demons—with anything that might get in the way of my creativity, my integrity, or pursuing my life's purpose or mission?

→ Have I been willing to stay in the struggle to find answers or best solutions—rather than cutting off the discovery process too early—in order to fully actualize the creative impulse?

→ How long am I willing to stay in the struggle, the "not knowing," and to count on the best answers to come?

→ Am I willing to stay in the struggle with other people who are working toward staying in the process, knowing that confusion, giving in, losing oneself, and conflict may be part of discovering the best answers?

→ How tolerant am I of ambiguity and risk?

→ Have I frequently set up intentional creativity time in which we stay in the discovery process for a while?

Perfect Phrases to Ignite Your Own Passion and Creativity

Answers Exist—What Might I Do Right Now, Today, to Increase My Belief That:

→ Answers already exist?

→ There are many possible answers?

→ There are creative ideas out there to discover?

→ All I have to do is search and I will find many possible solutions?

→ There are millions of ideas out there and I need just one or two of them?

→ Ideas are not hard to find?

→ The more ideas I come up with, the better?

→ If I listen carefully, I will hear many possibilities?

→ There is an eternal source of answers to tap into?

➜ I can dip my net into a source and come out with many answers?

➜ Solutions can be created by combining and borrowing what's already out there?

➜ The creative search for answers is a way of life?

➜ I can participate in that way of life?

➜ I can free up my own creativity?

Flow or Calling

➜ I am going to bring myself into greater harmony with what is meaningful to me.

➜ I need to hear and listen to something that is larger than myself, a higher power.

➜ I plan to connect regularly with what is creative within me.

➜ I am tuning in to where my inner vision is leading me.

➜ I will get in touch with my inner vision.

➜ I need to do more detaching from what is external so as to connect with what is internal.

➜ I am going to take the leap of faith to stop doing what I have always done and thinking what I have always thought.

➜ I need to get a clearer sense of what seeing my vision, being in the flow, following my call, or surrendering to the creative source looks like.

➜ I want to look for what gives me the greatest joy.

➜ Who am I?

➜ I need to focus on my center.

➜ I want to get clear on what is left when all the materialism of my life is stripped away.

➜ I am going to invest in discovering my purpose in life.

➜ I know what my purpose in life is, and I need to stay focused on it.

→ I am most happy and fulfilled when I am doing

  _____.

→ I am determined to invest in what gives me the greatest joy.

→ I am most creative when I experience the greatest harmony in my life.

→ I believe that God will direct me in the way I am to go and what I am to discover.

→ I will ensure that I stay in harmony with God and my calling.

→ I will listen to what my higher self tells me.

→ I will surround myself with positive influences and tune out the negative.

→ I care about creativity for many reasons.

→ I need to have faith during the creative process.

→ I want to focus on what and whom I really care about.

→ I am going to get in touch with what makes my heart sing.

→ I plan to stay connected with my calling, my center, the meaning of my life.

→ I am going to stay focused on what I can do to get into the flow and to stay open.

→ Values need to stay central in my decisions.

→ I am going to listen to what my higher self is saying right now.

→ If I visualize my higher self, I can better know what I should be doing or what direction I should go.

→ I am going to take a half hour to relax or meditate so as to regenerate my creative juices.

→ I am going to go somewhere quiet to see what answers I hear.

→ I need to empty myself, meditate, and focus internally so as to hear from my center.

→ I want to listen for the still, small voice inside.

→ I want to do what I love and love what I do.

→ I am going to follow my heart.
→ I am committed to delving deep into my purpose.
→ I want my work to reflect who I am.
→ I have discovered my purpose in life, and I am going to live it out.
→ My soul is speaking, and I am going to follow its leading.
→ I want the work I do to reflect my greatest purpose.
→ I plan to delve deeply into the creative source within me.
→ I know there is creativity inside me that I can tap into.
→ Follow the creativity. It is oxygen for the soul.
→ I am going to listen to what's at my core or to my higher power.
→ I know where I can find a source of abundance.
→ I plan to listen more to that source of abundance.
→ I plan to follow the power—the sense of being empowered when I am on the right path.
→ I know I need to follow my calling because it links me to others and empowers me.
→ Following my calling connects me to something that is greater than I am.
→ I plan to find and align with the creative power of the universe.
→ I know that the best change comes from a vision for the future.
→ I plan to pursue my vision to completion.
→ Day by day I listen more closely to the voice within.
→ If I meditate or do yoga, I will be able to hear that inner voice more clearly.

Valuing Myself

→ I want to take the bull by the horns to discover some new ideas.

→ I need to remember who I am and what I have accomplished so that I don't get discouraged.

→ I need to surround myself with people who believe in me.

→ I have done good work and accomplished much, and I will continue to do so.

→ I have confidence that I will come out on the other side of this.

→ I know that I will find better answers if I stick with it, gather good people around me, and stay open to the possibilities.

→ Every day in every way I am growing stronger and becoming more.

→ I have had many successful experiences, and I have developed the confidence that we will turn *this* into a success as well.

→ I know that I am creative and that I can create situations that stimulate creativity in myself and others.

→ My unique viewpoint will contribute to successful innovation.

→ The answer is out there, and I will find it or create it.

→ I am or will be able to judge which way to go at this crossroads—it may take some time, but that's okay.

→ I am sticking with this until I find an answer.

→ I know I can do it.

→ I have had good ideas before, and I will again.

→ I am going to take this idea by the horns and run with it until I get somewhere.

→ I want to investigate how I can increase my capacities, my strengths, and my value.

→ I am working to stay aware of myself, my thoughts, my feelings, my intentions, my values, and my choices.

→ I want to increase my sense of efficacy in the world—that is, the sense that I have personal power and can act on my choices.

→ I plan to add more creativity to my day-to-day life.

→ What might I do to add the characteristics of creative people to my life?

→ I am aiming for a new and productive attitude, that of approaching every workday as a creative endeavor.

→ I am carefully considering how I might see myself as more creative.

→ I need to think about how I can respond better to failure.

→ How can I conquer my fears?

→ I am going to challenge the things that interfere with my willingness to take risks.

→ I am determined to overcome the voice of judgment inside me.

→ I commit to valuing myself enough to take care of my body by exercising, eating right, and taking enough downtime.

→ I want to become more confident in myself and in my creativity.

→ I can accept my limitations, but, more important, I plan to overcome them.

→ I have the strength of commitment to endure defeat, lack of acceptance, and naysayers.

→ I am committed to my vision.

→ I have the strength of my convictions.

→ I know how to challenge the inevitable negative thoughts, and I plan to do so.

→ I believe that failure is part of success.

→ I will get back on the horse after any failure.

→ I trust in my creativity.

→ I will define myself as creative and as capable of creativity.

→ I will accept myself as I am and build toward getting better.

→ I will take good care of myself emotionally and relationally.

→ I trust my own intuition.

→ I am bold, tenacious, and committed to my ideas.

→ I will let go of perfectionism and give myself a break.

→ I accept my limitations, but I plan to stretch beyond them.

→ I refuse to be jealous of others' creative ideas because I am just as capable of being creative.

→ I am strong.

→ I commit to being true to myself.

→ I will find or create a safe space in which to express myself.

→ I am actively engaged in discovering myself.

→ I love myself.

→ I believe that creativity comes from within me, that I can locate it, and that I can catch it.

→ I have high, but not impossibly high, standards.

→ I am an independent person.

→ I am persistent in pursuing creative answers.

→ I see mistakes as opportunities to learn, rather than as embarrassments.

→ I will ward off the voice of judgment.

→ I refuse to be limited by fear.

→ I believe that I am smart, talented, and able to find many ideas.

→ I am dedicated and determined.

→ I have confidence in myself as a finder and creator of ideas.

→ I believe that I have access to a font of ideas.

→ I learn from my mistakes.

→ I know how to pick myself up and keep going.

→ I am a self-starter and am not overly reliant on other people.

- ➜ I am an actor, not a reactor.
- ➜ I follow through with my intentions.
- ➜ I affirm myself regularly.
- ➜ I can visualize myself as a success in creatively solving problems, and I use visualization regularly.
- ➜ I take downtime, or unstructured, unorganized time, because I know I need it.
- ➜ I take risks regularly.

Communities and Small Groups

- ➜ I am going to set up an innovation meeting for next week.
- ➜ I really need creativity meetings at least once a month.
- ➜ I am going to find people that can I brainstorm with on this.
- ➜ I need to hear what others have to say.
- ➜ I want to be more truthful and open with others.
- ➜ If I'm running short on creative ideas, I need to bring in more and different people to help me.
- ➜ I will regularly put together creativity teams to solve problems.
- ➜ I will bring new hires into the creativity team and initiate them into the creativity group process.
- ➜ I plan to ensure that there is enough difference in my teams—difference in professions, departments, skills, interests, passions, cultures, temperaments, and knowledge.
- ➜ I want to generate lots of energy in our small-group innovation meetings.

Whole-Brain Thinking

- ➜ What would happen if . . .?
- ➜ I am going to step back from what is immediate to see what I can see.

→ I wonder how I can think about this differently.

→ What's the wildest solution I can come up with?

→ I am going to write down as many "wacky" ideas as I can in as little time as possible.

→ I am going to aim for 100 new ideas before I start deciding.

→ I will write down as many ideas as I can, no matter whether they make sense or not.

→ I am going to use different colors (or images, or random words) to trigger different thinking on this issue.

→ What wild and crazy ideas am I willing to consider?

→ I need to move beyond my own internal censor.

→ I am going to build new connections and yoke images together.

→ I need to ensure that I and my team engage in a holistic approach to finding solutions.

→ When I visualize a solution, what do I see?

→ I am going to listen to my dreams.

→ I'm going to draw a picture of some solutions.

Whole Self

→ I am going to count on more ideas coming to me if I
  → Take a walk outdoors.
  → Go to the gym.
  → Go dancing.
  → Get out the clay or crayons.
  → Cook a meal.
  → Talk with a friend.
  → Play with my children.
  → Dig in my garden.

→ I know I need to activate my less rational senses (e.g., heart, body, vision, and touch).

→ I am going to take a break and just think of nothing at all.

→ I regularly commit to letting my mind go into stream-of-consciousness thinking and to just listening.

→ I plan to use my intuition.

→ I am just going to sit still and listen.

→ I think I might do some relaxation or meditation exercises.

→ My New Year's resolution is to live a more balanced life.

→ What would be really fun and crazy to do right now?

→ Art might stimulate my nonrational mind, my feelings, or my intuition, and I need that right now.

→ I think it would help if I accessed my unconscious, the "transcendent," or my deeper self.

→ I commit to keeping myself healthy: mentally, physically, spiritually, interpersonally, and emotionally.

→ I want to keep my mind active.

→ If I shift my attention, move to a new location, or add something to my environment, it might trigger my creativity.

→ Rather than my brain, I am going to use my eyes (or ears or touch or intuition) to consider this issue right now.

→ I need a break to meditate, do yoga, or exercise in order to take care of myself.

Accessing "Child"

→ I want to experience more fun and play at work.

→ I am going to imagine what my children would do if they were here, what they would want to do, and what they would urge me to do.

→ I am going to think about how I can be more childlike as I approach this problem.

→ What is the point of doing this if I can't have fun?

→ I commit to increasing my joy and my playfulness.

→ Children are silly—let's make this project sillier.
→ What makes me afraid of silliness?
→ I am going to imagine I am watching children right now to see what they would be doing so that I can emulate it.
→ The naïveté of a child might really help me right now.
→ I need to find a good joke.
→ I commit to doing whatever it takes to get unfettered enough to behave like a child.
→ I need to be more illogical.
→ I am going to break the rules and have fun doing it!

Openness

→ I need to find people to talk with to get some different perspectives.
→ I am going to find some people who never agree with me to see what they might say.
→ I need to find someplace to access different kinds of input or information and different kinds of people.
→ I plan to figure out whom else I can talk with in order to find some ideas that I can build on.
→ There are lots of places where I can borrow ideas to combine.
→ I am sure there is someone who knows something that might help me with this problem.
→ I am going on a hunt for great ideas that are already out there.
→ I am going to be more open to new ideas.
→ I am going to find one new idea each day.
→ I welcome your ideas.
→ I plan to do one new, different, and nonroutine thing each day.

- ➡ Today is my day to do something that is out of the ordinary, out of my usual comfort zone.
- ➡ I am going to do a walk-around and try to see 10 things I haven't noticed before.
- ➡ I need to think about what I might do to tune in to and better listen to people.
- ➡ Listening well really helps me to pay attention to what's going on around me.
- ➡ What is one new thing that I can invent today?
- ➡ I want to really pay attention to what is going on around me, both at work and at home.
- ➡ I am going to try to hear everything around me as though I might be deaf tomorrow.
- ➡ I am going to try to see everything around me as though I might be blind tomorrow.
- ➡ My creativity will increase if I reach out and touch everything I pass, and really pay attention to how it feels.
- ➡ In each meeting today, I am going to find one new pattern or exception.
- ➡ I wonder where I can find some new and different smells.
- ➡ I need to find one new thing I can learn today (one new book, one new course, or one new bit of knowledge).
- ➡ I am going into the next meeting with 10 questions, however dumb I think they might be.
- ➡ There are no dumb questions—in fact, I'm going to come up with 20 "dumb" questions on this issue.
- ➡ This weekend, I am making a bucket list.
- ➡ Tomorrow, I am doing one thing on my bucket list.
- ➡ I'm going to the mall to watch people.
- ➡ I wonder how many new people I can meet at this next meeting (or at the bar, the party, or the church).

→ I'm going on a field trip around my city during one lunch period each week.

→ I think I will take a driving trip this weekend, just to see where I end up.

→ While I drive around, I am going to make a recorded list of as many ideas as I can think of based on what I see.

→ I am going to figure out how to discover what people want, like, or need.

→ I am going to bring what I know to the table, and yet stay open to new possibilities.

→ I plan to open my mind and become more curious.

→ What gets in the way of my adventurousness?

→ I want to make the most of all my senses each day.

→ I need to figure out how to stay out of ruts.

→ I am going to find out about trends by paying attention to junk mail, newspapers, conference announcements, radio stations, and television programs.

Process

→ I am going to stay in a "not knowing" place for as long as necessary.

→ I commit to staying in the process without coming to premature conclusions.

→ I am going to schedule regular innovation meetings because I know they are necessary to get to creative solutions.

→ I never know what will come out the other end, but I commit to going into the innovation meeting anyway.

→ I commit to staying open to the possibilities and open to what happens when all of us interact in this way.

→ I may not like this "no-man's-land" right now, but I am going to hang in there with it for a while yet.

→ I may have to visit the pits of despair before I find the mountains of hope.

→ I've been down this path before, and I have always come out on the other side—I just need to trust that it will happen this time as well.

→ I am feeling tremendously anxious, but I know that is part of the process.

→ I keep wondering how we are going to move ahead and come to a conclusion; I have to keep stopping myself in order to stay in the moment.

→ I know that my greatest creativity comes from the most anxiety-producing moments, but that doesn't mean I have to like it.

→ Staying open to the process and staying in the process requires faith on my part; I know this to be truth, even if it is hard.

→ Something happens in "the between" when I talk with other people—I find it takes a lot of trust to stay there and wait for the creativity to happen.

Perfect Phrases to Encourage Others' Creativity

Answers Exist—What Can I Do to Help You Believe and Act as Though . . .

→ Answers already exist?

→ There are many possible answers?

→ There are creative ideas out there to discover?

→ If you search, you will find many possible solutions?

→ There are millions of ideas out there?

→ You need just one or two good ideas?

→ Ideas are not hard to find?

→ There are many possibilities if you just listen carefully?

→ There is an eternal source of answers to tap into?

→ You can dip your net into a source and come out with many answers?

→ Solutions can be created by combining and borrowing what's already out there?

→ The creative search for answers is a way of life?

→ You can participate in that creative way of life?

→ You can free up your own and others' creativity?

Supportive Environment

→ I am going to do my best to encourage your creativity.

→ Let's evaluate how helpful our working environment is in encouraging your creativity and innovation.

→ I want to ensure that we provide you with enough time and financial resources to be as creative as you need to be.

→ Let's carefully evaluate whether the resources allotted to you are adequate and are doing the job, so that you can be intentional about being creative.

→ Please let me know if I need to find you some more resources.

→ I am working on being a more accepting person so that you can feel freer to explore and fail and experiment.

→ I am trying to be less judgmental and critical so as not to hinder your creativity.

→ I am going to listen first, rather than critiquing first.

→ Please come to me with any new ideas you have.

→ I want to encourage you to experiment and try new things.

→ I am going to be more positive, supportive, and accepting.

→ Let's work to stop the internal voices of judgment or criticism that hamper your creativity.

→ I am going to be your greatest cheerleader when you come to me with new ideas.

→ I trust you to do your best, to explore, and to pick yourself up from failures.

→ Please let me know when you need input; otherwise, I will leave you to your own devices.

→ Why don't you go play around with this and have some fun?

→ I think I have been pressuring everyone too much. Let's talk about how I can relieve some of the pressure.

→ I want us to talk about what's going to float your boat here, what's going to make you happy.

→ Let's free up some time so that you can consider as many options as you need or want to.

→ I want to get clear on whether you have enough time to explore what captivates your imagination, even if it isn't related to a current product line.

→ I noticed you really having fun while working on _____. Let's talk about how you can bring that joy into your other projects, as well as what other projects might trigger that kind of fun for you.

→ Mistakes happen. If they don't, you aren't trying hard enough. So just get up and try again.

→ You have nothing to fear from me—I want you to "take off" and give it your all.

→ Break all the rules as you think about what we might do.

→ I want to hear the good and the bad.

→ I want you out there exploring, seeing the world, and considering all kinds of possibilities.

→ I am just as curious as you are to see what you come up with.

→ There is no such thing as a dumb question; I will ask many of them. I want you asking as many as you can think of.

→ I want you to ensure that you fail sometimes—if you don't, you aren't considering enough options or trying hard enough.

→ I want you to come to each meeting with 50 ideas; that's how I will know you are creating.

→ Okay, so I blew it here; let's figure out what direction to go in now.

→ I want to hear about all your mistakes—that's the only way you and I will learn what works and what doesn't.

→ Let's both of us consider all the assumptions we are making on this project or decision, and challenge them one at a time.

→ We might be wrong here; that doesn't mean we shouldn't try it, but let's think about what to do if we are wrong.

→ Let's have a backup plan in case we are wrong.

→ Here's the research on market needs—please generate as many ideas as possible about how we might respond.

→ Okay, I am clearly not getting you answers/resources fast enough; I am going to bring in _____ to help us out.

Flow or Calling

→ You need to have some fun.

→ Let's talk about what really matters to you and gives your life and work meaning.

→ I would like you to tune in to what your heart is telling you.

→ Let's carefully consider what values are guiding us at this point and which ones really matter.

→ I would really like you to listen carefully to what your insides are telling you.

→ I think it is important for you to connect with your center.

→ Let's talk about what you really care about.

→ I'd like you to consider whom you are doing all of this for.

→ Let's think about what really makes your heart sing.

→ I want you to do whatever you usually do to get into the flow.

→ What values stimulate your thinking?

→ Let's listen to the voice of your higher self right now.

→ It's that time again: time to relax or meditate so as to get clear on what's important.

→ I would like you to listen to what that still, small voice inside is telling you.

→ I love that you love working on this project; I know that means we have the best chance of finding some good answers.

→ Your enthusiasm tells me that we are on the right track.

→ How does what you are working on fit with what you really want to be doing?

→ Just take some time and listen to what that little voice inside of you is saying.

→ This project seems to fit well with who you are and what really matters to you.

→ Let's consider which of these projects gives you a greater sense of meaning or purpose.

→ I believe that there is a creative source within you. I would like to think with you about how you might tap into that source or how often you surrender to that creative source.

→ I believe that creativity is oxygen for our souls.

→ I listen to what's at my core or to my higher power. What about you?

→ I believe that there is a source of abundance out there for you to tap into.

→ How might you listen to that abundance, or listen to it more frequently?

→ Let's think about how you might do more of what you feel called to do, and about whether any part of this job fits with that calling.

→ I notice that when you do _____, you really seem as though you are "on" and in the flow.

→ Get out of the way and let the creative force work through you.

→ See if you can get aligned with the creative energy of the universe as you work on this project.

→ Let's ensure that you have a vision for the future or for change.

→ I want you to stand up for your vision even in the face of challenge.

→ I hope you will listen carefully to that still, small voice within you.

→ Have you ever used concentration techniques like meditation and yoga to empty yourself, to focus internally, to quiet your mind, to focus on your heart's leading, or to focus on your highest reality?

Helping Others Value Themselves

→ You do great work!

→ You have many good ideas.

→ You have brought many new ideas to the table in the past.

→ I have great confidence in you.

→ I know you will get past this hurdle.

→ Let's talk about what usually helps you in these situations or when you get stuck.

→ I want you to have people you can consult with who bring out the best in you.

→ Just take the bull by the horns and go for it. What do you have to lose?

→ Let's make sure you are surrounded by people who help you to believe in yourself.

→ You will come out on the other side. Never fear!

→ Many people believe in you. Keep that in mind.

→ You have contributed so much over the years. I know you will continue to do so.

→ You are a very creative [insert some other positive characteristics] person. Use that creativity.

→ Keep giving me your viewpoint. I need to hear it.

→ You will find the answer—it is out there waiting for you.

→ I know you can do it.

→ You have had great ideas in the past, and you will have them again in the future.

→ Stick with it. You will find an answer.

→ Look far into the future and visualize things that might be.

→ Let's consider how you might see yourself as more creative.

→ I'd like us to figure out how you can be less critical of your own ideas.

→ How do you take care of yourself (exercising, eating right, and taking enough downtime) so that your creativity can flourish? Do you need to do better at it?

→ I am confident in you and your creativity. Are you?

→ Sure you have limitations. We all do. Just work on overcoming them.

→ Yep, this is a defeat. They happen. They will continue to happen. Let's rise above it and move on.

→ You just have to keep on trying, whether others accept your ideas or not; there will always be naysayers, and you can't let them shake your commitment to your vision.

→ I am counting on the strength of your convictions.

→ Challenge those inevitable negative thoughts!

→ Failure is part of success.

→ It's time to get back on the horse!

→ Do you trust your creativity? I do.

→ I'd like you to define yourself as creative. That's the first step in becoming creative.

→ It's time for you to accept yourself.

→ I want you to focus on how to take care of yourself emotionally and relationally.

→ Trust your own intuition!

→ Be bold, tenacious, and committed to your ideas!

→ Perfectionism rarely works. Give yourself a break!

→ Accept your limitations, and aim to stretch beyond them.

→ Why be jealous? She came up with a good idea. You will have the next one.

→ Let's hone in on what your true self is telling you.

→ I want this to be a safe space in which you express yourself freely.

→ Let's ensure that you are actively engaged in discovering yourself.

→ Creativity comes from within you. I have confidence that you can find it.

→ Let's pursue high standards, be persistent, and develop independence.

→ Mistakes are opportunities to learn. There's no need to be embarrassed.

→ Keep several projects going. That way you will always feel good about something.

→ Don't judge yourself so harshly. Judgment hampers creativity.

→ I'd like to help you consider what will get you over your fears.

→ I want you to believe that you are smart, talented, and able to find many ideas.

→ We need dedicated and determined people like you working here.

→ I have confidence in you as a finder and creator of ideas.

→ I know that inside you somewhere is a fount of ideas.

→ Just learn from your mistakes, because you are going to make them.

→ You just have to pick yourself up and keep going.

→ I'd like to see you be an actor rather than a reactor.

→ I want to see follow-through.

→ Visualize yourself as a success in creatively solving the problem.

→ Take some downtime to care for yourself and do nothing.

→ Keep trying. Hang in there. Be persistent.

→ Take some risks.

Communities and Small Groups

→ Creativity and success are not solo activities.

→ Generating ideas works better with a team; why don't you find a few other people to talk with about this?

→ There is magic in connections with others; find some people and build those connections.

→ You never know what will come out of a lunch or a night out with a friend.

→ We are not solo operators; we need to build relationships that will stimulate us and help us.
→ Who can be your co-journeyers on this?
→ Speak it. Say it out loud—to someone.
→ Of course other people may be doing it. But what is unique about what you do because you are you?
→ Get some input from other people.
→ Let's consider whom you can brainstorm with about this.
→ If you want the best input, you will have to be truthful.
→ What would your mom tell you if she were here?
→ If you are running short on creative ideas, bring in more and different people to help you.
→ I want us to consider what team you could create to help you solve this problem.
→ We have some new hires. Why don't you ask a couple of them to join you in brainstorming some ideas?
→ Make sure you put together a group with enough different talents and experiences (different professions, departments, skills, interests, passions, cultures, temperaments, and knowledge).
→ Make sure your group has enough energy to create new ideas.

Whole-Brain Thinking

→ What would happen if . . . ?
→ Let's consider how you might think about this differently.
→ Let's step back from what is immediately apparent to see what you can see.
→ Let's spend a few minutes brainstorming possibilities.
→ I want us to focus on the wildest ideas you can come up with.

→ Let's write down as many wacky ideas as we can in as little time as possible.
→ Write down as many ideas as you can, whether they make sense or not.
→ The entrance ticket to our next creativity meeting is a list of 100 ideas.
→ If you think of this situation from a red perspective, what do you become aware of? (Shift colors or images, or use random words.)
→ There are many ideas out there. Are you considering as many of them as you can?
→ Let's figure out how to get your creative process to be free-wheeling enough.
→ I'd like you to consider what your dreams might tell you if you kept track of them.
→ Try using visualization and drawing some pictures to trigger your creativity.

Whole Self

→ Why don't you take a break from thinking about this and
  → Take a walk outdoors.
  → Go to the gym.
  → Draw your ideas.
  → Go have lunch with the gang.
→ Let's ensure that you include your heart (or your body, vision, or touch) in the idea-generating process.
→ Just take a break and think of nothing at all.
→ Let's start a stream-of-consciousness conversation.
→ I think it might help if you were to relax or meditate, since you seem to be stuck (or overly stressed).

→ Let's ensure that you live a balanced life so that you can access more than your head in coming up with ideas.

→ I would like you to consider how something like yoga might help you right now.

→ Just shift gears entirely and read something new and interesting that is unrelated to the problem at hand.

→ Find a place to sit and feed your soul for a while, and give up trying to think about this.

→ Listen to your gut.

→ Listen to your intuition.

→ How might you ensure that your emotional, spiritual, and physical self is optimally taken care of this year?

Accessing "Child"

→ Are you having fun yet?

→ Let's have some fun with this.

→ I want some joy in this problem-solving process.

→ We are going to consider what would be really fun and crazy to do right now.

→ Let's play some crazy games and see what they trigger.

→ I think we need to be more playful.

→ Imagine that your child is trying to solve this—what would he or she think?

→ Do you know any good jokes?

→ Let's think about what would make you laugh right now and how it might help in solving this problem.

→ Just feel free to laugh right out loud!

→ If you aren't laughing, your ideas aren't wacky enough.

→ Just be as illogical as you would like to be.

Openness

→ Tell your dream to five people from an array of backgrounds, life experiences, ages, and/or regions. Have each of them write the story of your success.

→ I recommend that you meet with some others to get as many different perspectives as possible.

→ Let's consider what someone who never agrees with you might say.

→ I would like you to think about what other sources of information you might access.

→ I recommend that you talk with some people who have ideas that you might borrow and build on.

→ Creative use of others' ideas is just as important as generating your own. Let's ensure that you have done the research to see what good ideas are out there.

→ Let's get open to new ideas.

→ I'd like you to think about one new, different, and nonroutine thing you could do today.

→ Walk around the building and see how many things you can see that you have never seen before.

→ Spend a little time really listening to the people around you. See what you haven't been hearing.

→ Do a walk-around and use your eyes as if tomorrow you will be blind. See what you discover.

→ Let's see what happens if you use your ears as if tomorrow you will be unable to hear.

→ Do you ever touch things as though you soon might not be able to feel anything?

→ Walk around the building, smelling everything you can. See if you come up with anything new.

→ Stay in the moment so that you can be completely aware of what's going on around you.

→ Walk through the office and see if you notice any exceptions and patterns to the problem.

→ I want you to take a course on something outside your field or read a new book.

→ Take an hour and walk around the office asking all kinds of questions—use a recorder.

→ Think about the dumbest questions that you could ask right now.

→ I want to know what piques your curiosity.

→ You need a "bucket list." Think about what ought to go on your list and let me see it.

→ See if you can meet five new people today.

→ See how much new information you can find today.

→ Try turning things over in your mind, turning the world upside down, or viewing the world differently.

Process

→ Just stay open to as many new ideas as possible.

→ Trust the process—there's no need to draw conclusions yet.

→ See if you can stay in the "not knowing" place for a while longer.

→ This "not knowing" place is uncomfortable, but from the depths of despair often come great answers.

→ You know how the process works—it is the pits for a while when you are in it. But the thrill on the other side is worth sticking it out.

→ Find a quiet, comfortable, and/or beautiful place to just sit and listen—see what comes.

➜ I can understand that you are feeling anxious, but you know that is part of the process.

➜ You keep wondering how we are going to move ahead and come to a conclusion; just keep stopping that thought and staying in the moment.

➜ You know that the greatest creativity comes from the most anxiety-producing moments; I can certainly understand that you might not like it.

➜ Staying open to the process and staying in the process require faith; you know that, even if it is hard.

➜ It is okay to feel uncomfortable while we're in the process.

Leaders' Phrases When They Are Succeeding at Creativity

➜ I love this work!

➜ Life is great!

➜ Aren't dreams terrific!

➜ Wild is good! Wacky is better!

➜ What a joy to create!

➜ My whole self is operating when I am creating.

➜ I am happiest when I acknowledge all parts of myself.

➜ I truly have a sense of being called when I am creating.

➜ I am in the flow!

➜ I am on a roll!

➜ This really matters!

➜ We did it!

➜ I am celebrating tonight!

➜ These creative ideas are coming from my center.

➜ I have a terrific group of people to work with.

➜ I love our creative interactions.

- → It's unbelievable how much comes out of our creativity meetings.
- → I trust the creative process.
- → I have such confidence in my team. We will do this!
- → I have confidence in myself!
- → We are going to lead the way with innovative ideas!
- → Our company is thinking well into the future.

CHAPTER 2

Motivating Teams to Be Highly Creative

Teams are critical to the creative process in most companies and organizations. Effective leaders realize this, and so they invest considerable amounts of time, energy, and money in developing, using, and motivating creativity and innovation teams. Innovative organizations and leaders encourage creativity by:

- Intentionally encouraging time for creativity meetings
- Ensuring that innovation teams are effective
- Creating an open, informal, free environment
- Creating an environment in which creativity and innovation are valued, reinforced, sought, and supported, rather than criticized or punished
- Providing mentors who know how to support people and stimulate creativity
- Acknowledging and valuing the "whole person" of each employee
- Tuning in to whether the environment external to the organization will support creativity and innovation (for example, it may be necessary to hunker down and become more self-protective during wars and recessions)

- Not supervising too closely
- Not placing constraints on creative time or on the range of possible solutions

The most creative teams value diversity and openness, and so effective leaders of innovation intentionally seek out differences in culture, opinion, temperament, personality, and talent when creating teams. Edward de Bono's Six Thinking Hats strategy, for instance, recognizes that people often play different roles and that each of these roles is valuable at certain times in a decision-making process. Different-colored hats (for example, red hats, black hats, and yellow hats) represent roles such as being visionary, looking for positives, or critically evaluating the possibilities. Instead of shutting down the people who are playing these roles (because we prefer other hats or because we really don't like people who wear certain hats), de Bono points to the value of each of the six hats, believing that leaders and managers ignore a particular hat to their detriment. He encourages leaders to recognize different hats or to assign people to play different roles so as to ensure that all angles are considered before decisions are made. The need for diversity may even move beyond people and roles to conducting innovation meetings in different physical locations. Intentionally moving meetings to different venues may get people "out of the box" and into creativity.

Mark Vamos, David Lidsky, and Jim Collins, in *Fast Company's Greatest Hits*, point out that leaders of creative and innovative teams and organizations consider the "larger issues of life" to be just "as important as the demands of profit-and-loss performance," and so, they create a "human organization":

- Putting values first
- Valuing people
- Offering love, caring, and support to "stretch" people into taking risks

- Considering trust to be central
- Empowering their employees
- Celebrating collaboration and mutual decision making
- Keeping fear and negativity to a minimum
- Eliminating destructive competition
- Flattening hierarchies
- Reducing bureaucracy
- Sharing openly about finances

As Michael Ray and Rochelle Myers point out in *Creativity in Business*, creative organizations make the working world a "celebratory arena rather than a bloody one," one that is more like a family. They indicate that creativity-inducing leaders:

- See their people as their most important advantage.
- Create and communicate a vision that people can believe in.
- Guide their people toward that vision.
- Help people and teams to develop skills serially and painlessly.
- Develop their workers' concentration, efficiency, accuracy, humor, and intuition.
- Emphasize how to learn new things and how to develop and express insights.

As a result, according to David Golman, Paul Kaufman, and Michael Ray in *The Creative Spirit*, the organization "becomes a complex, living organism, guided by a lively intelligence that needs to be continually stimulated."

Successful innovation teams also maximize the synergy among people. They value what happens when a group of different people intensively poses questions, struggles with potential answers, and generates ideas. Creativity-inducing leaders and managers use the power of interactions among different people, the "more" that happens in the energy of a group of different people who are working together on something that matters. These leaders create a group innovation process that is intentional, structured, and safe, but also fun and fulfilling. They help groups to assess their capacities and plans, and then to create the best conditions for innovation. And, finally, leaders, managers, and supervisors hire and reward creative people.

Perfect Phrases to Communicate Openness to Ideas and People

→ No idea is a bad idea. And even bad ideas may lead to good ideas.
→ We love new ideas.
→ We don't put people down.
→ You are very welcome here.
→ We will support you in any way we can.
→ Let's welcome Adib to our team!
→ Creativity lives here.
→ Bring your whole self to the table.
→ Your opinion matters.
→ The more different ideas we come up with, the better.
→ We want to hear from you.
→ Your ideas matter.
→ We hired you to contribute—don't hold back.
→ Let's not stomp on anyone.
→ Let's welcome the new member of our team.
→ Please make Annie welcome.
→ We can't wait to hear your ideas.
→ What gifts do you bring to this discussion?

→ I know you have talents that we will benefit from.

→ We welcome different thinking.

→ Let's be very clear about our openness to new ideas.

→ I want us to hear one another.

→ How can we ensure that everyone feels free to contribute?

→ Behaving badly results in failing to discover new and creative solutions.

→ How do we create an environment in which people feel safe to share?

→ What great ideas are already out there?

→ How open are we to new ideas?

→ I want everyone to find one new idea each day.

→ I welcome your ideas.

→ Let's plan to do one new, different, and nonroutine thing each day.

→ What can we do today that is out of the ordinary and out of our usual comfort zone?

→ I want each of you to do a walk-around and try to see 10 things you haven't noticed before.

→ Listening well really helps us to pay attention to what's going on around us.

→ What is one new thing you can invent today?

→ Let's really pay attention.

→ I'd like each of us to try to see everything around us as though we might be blind tomorrow.

→ What would happen to our creativity if we reached out and touched everything we passed, and really focused on how it felt?

→ I wonder where we can find some new and different smells.

→ I want each of you to ask yourself, "What's one new thing I can learn today (one new book, one new course, or one new bit of knowledge)?"

➜ I want each of you to come to the next meeting with 10 questions, however dumb you think they might be.

➜ There are no dumb questions—in fact, I want each of you to come up with 20 dumb questions on this issue.

➜ This weekend, let's all make a bucket list.

➜ Tomorrow, I want each of us to plan how to do one thing on his or her bucket list.

➜ Let's go to the mall to watch people.

➜ I want to challenge you to meet as many new people as you can at this next meeting (or conference).

➜ We're going on a series of field trips around the city during one lunch period each week.

➜ While we're on these trips, I want each of you to make a list of as many ideas as you can think of based on what you see.

➜ Let's find out what people want, like, or need.

➜ How can we bring what we know to the table and stay open to new ways of arranging what we know?

➜ We need to open our minds and become more curious.

➜ What gets in the way of our being really adventurous as we approach work and think of new ideas?

➜ Let's make the most of all of our senses each day.

➜ Let's go around the circle and say what we do to get out of ruts.

➜ Let's pay attention to trends that are evident in our junk mail, newspapers, conferences announcements, and radio and television programming.

➜ Tell your dream to five people from an array of backgrounds, life experiences, age groups, and regions. Record their responses.

➜ Let's meet with some others to get as many different perspectives as possible.

➜ Let's consider who never agrees with us and what he or she might say.

→ I'd like us to access other sources of information for ideas that we can borrow and build on.

→ Creative use of others' ideas is just as important as generating our own.

→ What have we done to discover the good ideas that are out there?

→ Let's spend a little time really listening to the people around us. Let's see what we haven't been hearing.

→ Let's use our ears as if tomorrow we will be unable to hear.

→ We should go out and touch things as though we soon might not be able to feel anything.

→ Let's consider how well we do at staying in the moment and becoming completely aware of what's around us.

→ Walk through the office and see if you notice any exceptions or patterns to the problem.

→ I want you to take a course in something outside your field, or read a new book.

→ Take an hour and walk around the office asking all kinds of questions—use a recorder.

→ What piques your curiosity?

→ See if you can meet five new people today.

→ See how much new information you can find today.

→ Try turning things over in your mind, turning the world upside down, or viewing the world differently.

→ Let's ensure that we are allowing our ethics and values to affect our ideas and the range of ideas that we are considering. How might we do this? In what way could this be helpful?

→ I want us to ensure that we are exposing ourselves to a broad range of social ideas, minority views, and new information.

Perfect Phrases to Generate Buy-In (for the Creativity Process)

→ Creativity is necessary for innovation.

→ Creativity is fun!

→ Creativity isn't a gift; it's a process that everyone can participate in.

→ Creativity is about borrowing ideas and combining them into new solutions.

→ Innovation is necessary in today's world of fast-paced change.

→ We need to be innovative if we are to compete in the marketplace today.

→ Incremental improvements and problem solving are important, but they are not enough.

→ Creativity and innovation move us beyond incremental improvements and problem solving.

→ Our regular meetings haven't generated the ideas we need. Let's try something different.

→ de Bono [or another creative innovator] has had great success with using the Six Thinking Hats [or name another creativity exercise]. Let's try that now.

→ Remember how successful it was when we [name an idea-generating event]—let's try that in this situation.

→ The green team came up with 100 new ideas in its last meeting. Let's see if we can do even better.

→ Wouldn't you like to be excited by the possibilities?

→ Let's have some fun!

→ What really matters to you? Let's work together to make it happen.

→ Let's see how many of us can get into the flow.

→ We want to do something really meaningful here.

→ Let's think out into the future—where would we like to be in 10 years? What will really matter to us then?

→ Let's not be satisfied with the status quo. Let's reach for the stars!

→ Enough is never enough.

→ Let's think like winners, like world changers!

→ Let's each choose a genius (such as Benjamin Franklin or Bill Gates) and approach this meeting the way that person would.

→ We've got the basics. Now let's build them into something that really matters, something that we will be proud to hand down to our children.

→ The best answers come when we use and celebrate all parts of ourselves, everything that we can bring to the table. Let's get in touch with that.

→ We're not settling for less than the best!

→ We're no longer going to be reactive—we're going to get out in front and lead the pack.

→ We are going to be proud to stand behind our new product line.

→ We will go far!

→ Don't you want to do something that really matters in this world?

→ What will really give your life and work meaning?

→ Wouldn't you rather have your work be meaningful, something that you love doing and can be proud of?

→ Let's make our mark on the world!

→ Let's imagine what we could do if we really thought outside the box.

→ Imagine what it would be like if you could go as far as you would like to go with this company, with your great ideas.

Perfect Phrases to Stimulate the Team's Self-Assessment (of Its Creativity or Creative Potential)

Answers Exist

→ Do we believe that:
- → Answers already exist?
- → There are many possible answers?
- → Creative ideas are out there to discover?
- → All we have to do is search and we will find many possible solutions?
- → There are millions of ideas out there, and we need just one or two of them?
- → Ideas are not hard to find?
- → The more ideas we come up with, the better?
- → If we listen carefully, we will hear many possibilities?
- → There is an eternal source of answers to tap into?
- → We can dip our nets into that source and come out with many answers?
- → Solutions can be created by combining and borrowing what's already out there?
- → The creative search for answers is a way of life?
- → We can free up our own creativity?

→ What works best for us in generating creative responses to the current changes in our business environment?

→ What has been the most successful strategy we have found for generating actionable ideas?

Supportive Environment for One Another

→ Do we ensure that we have enough time to explore what captivates our imagination, even if it isn't related to a current product line?

→ Do we pay attention to what we enjoy, allowing one another some latitude to explore in those areas?

→ Do we try to find out what our team members enjoy?

→ Are we understanding of one another when mistakes happen?

→ Do we encourage one another to try enthusiastically, knowing that failures are part of success?

→ Do we actively try to reduce one another's fear?

→ Are we overly concerned with conformity to rules and standards?

→ Do we invest in innovation?

→ Are we open to all kinds of input?

→ Are we curious?

→ Do we encourage curiosity in one another?

→ Do we encourage questioning?

→ Do we encourage one another to try ideas that fail in order to find those that work?

→ Do we learn from past failures and expect the rest of the team to do the same, rather than making the same mistakes over and over?

→ Are we suspicious of low failure rates, deeming them evidence of not taking enough risks or of hiding mistakes rather than learning from them?

→ Are we willing to challenge our assumptions?

→ Do we plan for being wrong?

→ Are we prepared to change our execution plans?

→ Do we know and communicate with one another about market needs?

→ Are we willing to strike out and have our team members strike out sometimes?

→ Do team members communicate that they trust one another?

→ Do team members accept one another?

→ Do team members refrain from being judgmental and critical, particularly when others are trying to be creative?

→ Do team members listen to one another first, rather than critiquing first?

→ How encouraging are team members when people come up with ideas?

→ Do team members challenge one another to be more positive, supportive, and accepting?

→ Do team members firmly stop voices of judgment or criticism?

→ Does our team have cheerleading sessions for particularly creative ideas?

Flow or Calling

Do we encourage our team members to:

→ Access what is larger than themselves?

→ Find the flow?

→ Pursue peak experiences?

→ See their work as a vocation or a "calling"—something that is very central to their life and identity?

→ Ask one another questions about the meaning of life and work?

→ Take time out for reflection?

→ Connect with what is "higher" in life?

→ Pursue what is centrally important to them?

→ Listen to their own center, so as to hear the "still, small voice" inside?

→ Love what they are doing?

→ Do things they are enthusiastic about?

→ Operate from their center?

→ Find an integration between their work and who they are?

→ Bring their souls to work?

→ Be themselves?

→ Live out their life's purpose?

→ Stay connected with what gives their life meaning and purpose?

→ Discover the creative source within themselves and tap into it?

→ Surrender to that creative source?

→ Listen to the source of abundance that is out there to tap into?

→ Believe that creativity is oxygen for the soul?

→ Listen to what's at their core or to some higher power?

→ Believe that they are called?

→ Find their source of power when they are working on an idea?

→ Connect to something that is greater than they are?

→ Get out of the way and let the creative force work through them?

→ Take time out for reflection or quiet—to connect with what is "higher" in life and to align with the creative energy of the universe?

→ Find a vision for the future or for change?

→ Stand up for their vision even in the face of challenge?

→ Listen carefully to the voice within?

→ Use concentration techniques like meditation and yoga to empty themselves, to focus internally, to quiet their mind, to focus on their heart's leading, or to focus on their highest reality?

Team Identity and Strength

→ Are we a strong team that can accomplish anything we set our minds to?

→ Do we see our team as capable and able to make a difference?

→ Do we have a sense of power—do we feel strong enough to take action?

→ Are we committed to taking action?

→ Are we proactive rather than reactive in our pursuit of creativity and innovation?

→ Do we challenge the voice of judgment?

→ How confident are we in ourselves and in our creativity?

→ Do we know and accept our limitations? Do we try to overcome them?

→ Do we look to one another for help to tackle shortcomings?

→ Do we have the strength of commitment to endure many defeats, lack of acceptance, and naysayers? How committed are we to our vision?

→ Do we have the strength of our convictions?

→ Do we know how to challenge the inevitable negativity?

→ Do we believe that failure is part of success?

→ Can we get back on the horse after a failure?

→ Do we trust our creativity?

→ Are we bold, tenacious, and committed to our ideas?

→ Are we jealous of others' creative ideas? Or do we believe that we are just as capable of creating?

→ Do we have high standards?

→ Are we persistent in pursuing creative answers?

→ Do we see mistakes as opportunities to learn, rather than embarrassments?

→ Do we ensure that we have several projects going at once, rather than limiting our focus to one project?

→ Are we dedicated and determined?

→ Do we have confidence in ourselves as finders and creators of ideas?

→ Are we actors or reactors?

→ Are we persistent?

→ Do we take risks?

→ Do we have fun while doing it?

Whole-Brain Thinking

→ How many new and innovative ideas have we come up with in the last year?

→ When was the last time we successfully generated a rash of creative ideas in response to a problem we were facing?

→ To what degree are we engaging in activities that reach beyond our rational brains?

→ What's the ratio between how much we use our rational brains and how much we use our nonrational brains?

→ How frequently do we take breaks from our rational minds?

→ Do we always have to make sense?

→ How many different ideas do we come up with before we make a decision?

→ How novel, surprising, or unusual are the ideas that we come up with?

→ How many innovative strategies have we come up with in the past year?

- → How often are we in situations where we are dreaming up new ideas?
- → There are many ideas out there. Are we considering as many of them as we can?
- → Do we tune in to patterns and shadings?
- → Do we ensure that our creative process is freewheeling enough?
- → Do we use visualization or drawing pictures as part of creativity meetings?
- → How successful are we in building on other people's ideas?
- → How are we doing in finding ideas to borrow and combine?
- → How many new combinations have we come up with recently?
- → To what degree do we use both our right *and* our left brains?

Whole Self

- → How much of ourselves do we bring to the table when we are solving problems?
- → What role does intuition play in our innovation?
- → What roles do the unconscious, the "transcendent," or our deeper selves play in our innovation process?
- → How often do we use more holistic thinking and look at the big picture?
- → Are we exercising our physical bodies as well as our minds?
- → Do we keep ourselves healthy—physically, spiritually, interpersonally, and emotionally—so as to access these parts of ourselves when creating?
- → In what ways do we use the creative arts to stimulate our nonrational mind, our feelings, or our intuition?

→ To what degree do we take time out of the workday and take breaks in creativity team meetings for reflection or quiet?

→ How often do we try to daydream or remember our dreams in order to bring unconscious knowledge into creativity meetings?

→ During creativity meetings, are we honoring our happy, sad, angry, and/or fearful feelings by thinking about them, talking about them, and figuring out what to do about them?

→ How often do we encourage our team members to meditate, do yoga, or exercise in order to take care of themselves? Do we create space for these sorts of activities during innovation meetings or retreats?

→ Do we schedule walks or time out of the meeting room when we are trying to create?

→ How frequently do we change our environment in some dramatic way when we are trying to create—for example, go to the beach, to the park, skiing, to a beautiful retreat center, or to a children's playroom?

→ How often do we go somewhere peaceful to think and to observe?

→ How frequently do we shift the senses we are using as we are engaged in a creativity process?

→ Do we ask ourselves frequently enough about our gut reactions, or what our intuition tells us?

Perfect Phrases to Engage Team Creativity

Answers Exist—Let's Believe and Act As If:

→ Answers already exist.
→ There are many possible answers.
→ Creative ideas are out there to discover.
→ All we have to do is search and we will find many possible solutions.
→ There are millions of ideas out there, and we need just one or two of them.
→ Ideas are not hard to find.
→ The more ideas we come up with, the better.
→ If we listen carefully, we will hear many possibilities.
→ There is an eternal source of answers to tap into.
→ We can dip our nets into a source and come out with many answers.
→ Solutions can be created by combining and borrowing what's already out there.
→ The creative search for answers is a way of life.
→ We can free up our own creativity.

Leaders Creating a Supportive Environment

→ We have now developed metrics that reflect the quantity of ideas and outputs (prototypes built, patents filed, papers published, projects completed, and so on), since more ideas mean more success.
→ We want you to be as creative as possible. What can we do to support your creativity?
→ Let's talk about how to free up the team's creativity.

→ Let's consider the time and the financial and personnel resources you will need to have allocated for creativity and innovation meetings.

→ Are the resources I have allotted adequate? Are they doing the job?

→ Let's discuss whether I need to find more resources for your team.

→ I am not going to evaluate your ideas right now—just spend your time coming up with as many ideas as you can.

→ I want to encourage you to keep coming up with as many ideas as possible.

→ Let's talk about how our team can be more positive, supportive, and accepting and less judgmental and critical.

→ I commit to being less judgmental and critical and to challenging judgment when it interrupts creativity.

→ What can I do to encourage your team's creativity?

→ This Friday, we are celebrating all of our new ideas and the process we have gone through to come up with them.

→ I trust you all. I know you are working hard on new ideas. I have confidence that you will be truly creative.

→ I am going to check in with your team at the end of the week. But until then, you have the freedom to let your imaginations soar.

→ Make sure you have some fun—I put balloons, candy, games, and coloring materials in the back of the room to stimulate your creativity.

→ Let's talk about what I can do to reduce the pressure on the team or on individuals.

→ In today's meeting, I want to hear about the moment this year that was most powerful and inspirational for you here at work. Then, we're going to talk about how to create more of those moments.

→ Let's ensure that you have at least one afternoon a month away from the building to explore what captures your imagination.

→ Hey, mistakes happen. If you aren't making mistakes, you aren't really trying.

→ We are going to do some brainstorming at next week's meeting. I want you to bring 20 questions and 20 new ideas, no matter how dumb you might think they are.

→ I'd like to take some time to consider what we can learn from this idea that failed.

→ What assumptions are we making here? Do we need to challenge them?

→ Our first task here is to discover market needs. Let's do an explore and ask everyone we know to give us input.

→ This Friday afternoon, we are having a "bash" to celebrate all of the creative ideas we have come up with this month.

→ I want to ensure that everyone is working in an area or on a project that he or she can get excited about.

→ I want us to get in the flow as much as possible around here.

→ After Josephine presents her idea, I want us to ask her as many questions as possible, and we will record the questions. That will give her a great deal of input to think about.

Flow or Calling

→ Let's talk about what we really care about, what really matters to us.

→ It matters for whom we are doing all of this.

→ I'd like us to focus on what really makes us sit up and take notice.

→ If we thought with our hearts right now, what might we come up with?

→ We need to ensure that we get into and stay in the flow.

→ We will do best if we invest in what we would really love to do, as if money and time were no object.

→ Our creativity may be enhanced if we invest in something we really care about.

→ Let's consider how we can infuse values into our creativity process.

→ We need to consider what our higher selves are saying right now.

→ If we put our higher selves in the driver's seat right now, where would we go?

→ Let's take a break and take a walk on the beach (or in the park or in the woods) to see what answers we hear.

→ I'm going to lead us in a relaxation exercise so as to tap into what matters centrally to us.

→ Let's think about what part of this really matters.

→ If we brought the "transcendent" or our deeper selves into the room right now, what would we discover?

→ I want people to do what they love doing!

→ The best work comes from the heart, from what we are called to do.

→ As we generate ideas, let's keep the central focus on what we value.

→ Let's follow our enthusiasm.

→ I'd like each of you to tune in to what that still, small voice is telling you right now.

→ Let's bring our souls to work, to this project, and to the brainstorming process.

→ There is a creative source, a source of abundance, and we are going to figure out how to tap into it.

→ Let's keep our vision front and center.
→ Don't forget what we would really like to have happen here.

Sense of Team Identity and Strength

→ We have a terrific team to work with here.
→ We have the capacity to make a real difference.
→ If we decide and take action, no one can stop us.
→ We need to connect with our sense of power and get strong enough to take real action.
→ We are committed to taking action, and we have chosen the best direction in which to act.
→ From here on out, we are going to be proactive rather than reactive in creating action plans.
→ We are going to take time out from listening to the voice of judgment.
→ We should feel confident in ourselves and in our creativity. We have had many successes this year.
→ Let's identify our limitations and make decisions about how to overcome them.
→ We have the strength of commitment to endure many defeats, to endure lack of acceptance, and to endure naysayers.
→ We are committed to our vision. There's no stopping us now.
→ We are strongly committed to this endeavor.
→ Negativity may threaten our efforts, but we know how to beat it down.
→ Failure is part of success. The more failures, the more creativity.
→ We will simply get back on the horse whenever we fail, and we will have learned from the failure.

→ We trust our ability to come up with new and creative solutions.
→ We are bold, tenacious, and committed to our ideas.
→ We are just as capable of creating as anyone else, so we have no reason to be jealous.
→ We commit to having high standards.
→ We will be persistent in discovering creative answers.
→ Mistakes are opportunities to learn, not embarrassments.
→ We are dedicated and determined.
→ We are finders and creators of ideas.
→ We are actors rather than reactors.
→ We will be risk takers because that's how we will find the best ideas.

Whole-Brain Thinking

→ What would happen if . . . ?
→ How might we think about this differently?
→ Bring 100 new ideas to the next meeting.
→ Let's spend a few minutes brainstorming possibilities.
→ Let's generate as many ideas as we possibly can as quickly as we can. Let's not evaluate any of these ideas yet.
→ What are the wildest ideas we can come up with? Just shout them out as quickly as possible.
→ Let's write down as many "wacky" ideas as we can in as little time as possible. We'll figure out what is workable later.
→ Let's not make any decisions until we have as many ideas on the table as possible.
→ Let's step back a moment from what is immediately apparent. How might our perspectives change?

➜ We've been using our left brains a lot. Let's shift for a moment to our right brains and see things more holistically, emotionally, visually, and intuitively.

➜ Let's take a break from the rational and get a little crazy for a moment.

➜ It doesn't matter whether an idea makes sense. Just call out as many as you can.

➜ Perhaps if we draw pictures of our ideas, our ideas will be more creative.

➜ Create a picture of the way things are and the way you would like things to be.

➜ Let's write as many ideas as possible or that we know about, and then let's invite others to add to those ideas, rearrange them, or combine them.

➜ Visualize the color red—throw out any ideas that you associate with red [or change colors, or use images or random words].

Whole Self

➜ For innovation meetings:
  → Let's be sure to include activities that will trigger as many nonrational thoughts or experiences as possible.
  → I want to talk about how to ensure that the meeting location is inspiring.

➜ We seem to have hit an impasse. Why don't we take a break from thinking about this and:
  → Take a walk outdoors.
  → Go to the gym.
  → Go out to lunch.
  → Revisit this issue tomorrow.

➜ Let's take a break and just think of nothing at all.

→ Let's switch seats [or stand up if people are sitting; or move to a different location; or draw what we are talking about] as a way of taking on a different role or perspective.

→ Let's go somewhere and do something different from what we are doing now.

→ I want us to pay attention to our intuition and what it's telling us right now.

→ Let's talk with some people who have different expertise or interests.

→ Let's go somewhere different for a while, somewhere that stimulates a different part of our brains and our bodies.

→ Let's figure out ways to put our hearts (or our bodies, vision, or touch) into the idea-generating process.

→ I am going to lead us in a meditation exercise to see where relaxation and visualization will take us.

→ Let's draw a picture of how we would like things to be.

→ What would be really fun and crazy to do right now?

→ Let's build the energy by getting out of the room once in a while.

→ Consider what other parts of ourselves it might be helpful to bring to the table right now (for example, our heart, soul, or body).

→ Let's step back from the immediate, the small stuff, the analyzing, and see if we can imagine that we are looking at the situation from space and seeing the big picture, where all of this fits.

→ If we were all to put our bodies into a position that represented the problem, what would our positions or postures look like? Now, let's put our bodies into a position that represents the solution. What would it take to move from the problem position to the solution position?

→ Let's draw, write poetry, create a video, or engage in some other creative endeavor in order to understand this problem (or solution) better.

→ We're going to take 15 minutes to go for a walk, let our minds go blank, and just tune in to what we sense around us.

→ We are meeting again tomorrow. Before you go to sleep this evening, put a pad of paper and a pencil beside your bed. Ask a question about something we have been discussing today. When you wake up, write down what you dreamed. We will do some free association about the dreams and the issues as part of tomorrow's work.

→ Draw a picture with colors that express your feelings about what we are talking about.

→ Before dinner this evening, we are taking a half hour break for you to access your inner self—reflect, do yoga, take a walk, look at the sky, or exercise. Then jot down notes on what comes to you about the issues under discussion.

→ We are going to have a series of creativity Fridays, each one in a different place: the beach, the park, a ski resort, a retreat center, and a preschool.

→ What is your gut reaction? What is your intuition telling you?

Accessing "Child"

→ Let's keep the fun going by having groups present their ideas as humorous skits.

→ Perhaps groups will have more fun and thus generate more ideas if we make this process into a game with prizes.

→ Let's have more fun while we do this.

→ We need to laugh more. Talk to me about what will put smiles on our faces and laughter in our hearts.
→ Consider what we need to do to bring a sense of joy into our brainstorming about possible solutions.
→ Let's play—what games do you know? Let's bring those games into our creativity sessions.
→ Are we having any fun yet?
→ Tell me your most outrageous idea.
→ Let's put ourselves in our child's shoes as we try to solve this one and consider what a little kid might say.
→ Who knows a good joke?
→ Let's come up with illegal and immoral ideas, or ideas we could get fired for.
→ How might we bring more fun into our work more generally?

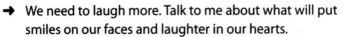

Perfect Phrases to Tap into Existing and Varied Expertise

→ We need to carefully consider whom to invite into the conversation so as to hear as many different perspectives as possible.
→ Let's ensure that we hear as many conflicting views as possible during our innovation meeting.
→ When we put our team together, let's make sure we have as much diversity of cultures, skills, opinions, talents, interests, and experiences as possible.
→ Let's make a list of everyone who is involved in this problem.

- → I want us to think about who disagrees with us, what those people would say, and how we can ensure that we take their opposition into consideration.
- → Let's role-play different sides of this conflict so that we hear all the possibilities.
- → Let's ensure that each of the departments or positions involved is represented at the meeting.
- → What expertise do we need at this meeting to ensure that we are coming up with the best answers?
- → Let's investigate who has had a similar problem and would have needed to come up with answers that we might find beneficial.
- → I want us to consider where we might borrow ideas to build on.
- → Let's assume that we don't know everything, and that each other person here knows something we need to know.
- → Let's each try on different hats [de Bono's hats: red, green, black, blue, and so on] to ensure that we are hearing different ways of thinking.
- → We need to trust one another to ensure that everyone will be heard, no one will be put down, and if we work together, we will come up with the best solutions.
- → Let's ensure that we have included people from each of the professions.
- → We have lots of introverts in our department—let's ensure that we include some extraverts in our creativity meetings.
- → How can we ensure that our group is diverse enough to represent a variety of different views?
- → We will need one of the researchers, one of the marketing people, and the head of finance to participate in this discussion.
- → Jerry has been here forever, so let's include him. But let's also include Sarah, the intern, Janica, one of our newer administrators, and Javier, the newest professional.

→ We need representatives on the team who have different kinds of information, different goals, different roles, and different experiences.

→ While in the process of creating, we need to expose ourselves to many different fields of study, many different experiences, many different cultures, and many different environments.

→ We need to become aware of the social, political, and cultural contexts that affect our team, our workplace, and our future as a company.

→ Let's ensure that we hear all kinds of different ideas and that we are respectful in the process.

→ I want to ensure that I hear everyone and hear all the possible ideas.

→ The best ideas come from lots of different people working together.

→ Sharon has particular gifts in this area.

→ Let's create a team of people who don't tend to agree with one another to make sure that we hear different perspectives.

→ Where might we go to access different kinds of input or information and hear from different kinds of people?

→ Let's think carefully about whom else we need to ask for ideas that we can build on.

→ Who knows something that might help us with this problem?

→ During our discussions, we need to access representatives with a wide range of talents, experiences, and cultures.

→ Let's consider carefully what we can do to attract people with different backgrounds into the discussion.

Perfect Phrases to Harness the Power of the Group

→ Let's consider how often we should meet together to generate new ideas.

→ We need to ensure that our team members support one another's ideas. How might we do that?

→ Let's talk about how to be cooperative and how to build a healthy group.

→ I know I can trust the process of creating with this group. We just have to stay with it for a while longer and trust one another.

→ Let's hold a creativity meeting to generate innovative ideas.

→ I think more people need to be in the room to create the best solutions.

→ I will send out the agenda or issue that we are facing ahead of time to ensure that people have time to reflect on it before the meeting.

→ Let's brainstorm as many possibilities as we can without, for the moment, evaluating any of them.

→ Let's make sure that everyone has a chance to be heard.

→ (Name) _____ , I haven't heard from you yet. I am wondering what you are thinking.

→ I have faith in what we can come up with as a team.

→ We aren't going to comment on any ideas yet.

→ Let's move as quickly as we can in generating ideas.

→ If your foot [or another body part] were speaking, what would it say?

→ If the stars were speaking, what would they say?

→ Let's stay with this process as long as possible, even if it's uncomfortable.

- ➜ I know the struggle is difficult, but eventually we will come out on the other side—let's not rush it.
- ➜ We have succeeded before, and we will succeed again. Let's trust one another.
- ➜ Is there anything that is hindering us as a group? Anything that we might improve on?
- ➜ Let's not cut off the ideas too quickly. Let's stick with the brainstorming as long as possible.
- ➜ We have many very smart and creative people here. Let's ensure that we hear what everyone has to offer, even if it gets tough at times.
- ➜ We need to include people who are energetic and moti- vated, rather than those who are merely waiting until retirement.
- ➜ How can we streamline the team so as to get the most done?
- ➜ Perhaps we can have many representatives but divide them up into small groups for brainstorming.
- ➜ Let's put the managers in one group so that those whom they manage will feel freer to contribute.
- ➜ Let's not put any direct reports in groups with their supervisors.
- ➜ Let's institute regular creativity and innovation meetings.
- ➜ We need to create and use teams regularly.
- ➜ Teams working together really add to the creative process.
- ➜ We need to create a team of people that trust one another, so that they can be fully truthful with one another while innovating.
- ➜ Cooperativeness (rather than competitiveness) is critical to our team's creativity.
- ➜ Let's consider how we might be more supportive, helpful, and encouraging toward one another.

→ I want to ensure that I am being supportive, helpful, and encouraging as a team leader. So, please give me feedback—now, later, in an e-mail, or anonymously.

→ If we are running short on creative ideas, let's bring in more and different people to help us.

→ Let's use the power of teamwork whenever we have a problem to solve.

→ We need to ensure that we add some new hires to our creativity team. Who would be best? Let's talk about how we will initiate them into the creativity group process.

→ Let's carefully consider how we might increase the energy in our small group meetings.

→ I need your input on whether we have wrestled with this issue long enough. Let's ensure that we are not cutting the struggle short just because it isn't easy.

→ Have we brainstormed long enough, or do we need to keep it going longer?

→ We keep ourselves struggling long enough with people or ideas or values or ambiguity or risk, even when it is uncomfortable or we can't see the light at the end of the tunnel.

→ We may need to bear the discomfort of not knowing for a while, rather than deciding before enough ideas are on the table.

→ We want the best solutions—and that requires hanging in there long enough.

→ Let's talk about how frequently we should schedule creativity and innovation meetings.

→ Let's begin by talking about how to make innovation meetings optimally effective.

→ Let's ensure that we are aiming for what is optimal as we generate large numbers of creative ideas.

- We will need to create different types of teams for different types of needs.
- Let's really be supportive, helpful, and encouraging of one another while we are creating.
- Speed kills the censor (of new ideas), so let's generate ideas as quickly as possible.
- There is an unlimited supply of ideas out there—if we stick with this process long enough, we will find the good ones.
- If creativity isn't a destination, but a journey, then let's consider what helps us stay on the journey, rather than closing it down.
- Talk to me about what you need to take on this journey into creativity.
- Let's start the journey, even if we don't know what the destination will be.
- It will take courage to stay in the process of discovery long enough.
- Staying in the discovery process often feels risky, but we can do it!
- Let's embrace our anxieties—they are vital to the creative process, even if we find them uncomfortable.
- Let's view this process as an adventure!

Perfect Phrases for Hiring Creative Employees

- We value creativity in our employees.
- Creativity is essential to our remaining competitive.
- All employees must fully activate their creative potential.
- Everyone is responsible for innovation.

→ Please prepare a demonstration or illustration of your creativity potential.

→ Please come to your interview with examples of innovations you have helped to create.

→ We will hold group interviews in which you will brainstorm to generate creative ideas for a particular market.

→ You will have the opportunity to observe creativity in process; we will ask you to evaluate what you see, identify key success factors, and make suggestions for improvement.

→ After having potential hires observe an innovation meeting, ask them:

   → What went well? What went poorly?
   → What would you change or improve on?
   → If you had been a participant, what ideas would you have thrown into the mix?
   → How would you feel if you had been a participant?
   → Have you participated in meetings such as this? Please describe.

→ Come to the interview with creative ideas for _____ (name the problem or situation).

→ Come to your interview prepared to brainstorm with others ideas for meeting the challenges of the current economy.

→ Please ensure that your résumé illustrates your creativity potential.

→ Please submit evidence of your creativity.

→ Your references need to be prepared to offer evidence of your creativity.

→ Check off and rank the top 10 of the following characteristics that apply to you:

   → Capable
   → Clever
   → Confident

→ Humorous
→ Individualistic
→ Informal
→ Insightful
→ Intelligent
→ Interested in many things
→ Inventive
→ Original
→ Reflective
→ Resourceful
→ Self-confident
→ Unconventional
→ Curious
→ Intrinsically motivated
→ Willing to take risks
→ Open to new experiences and ideas
→ Flexible behaviorally and cognitively
→ Bold
→ Nonconformist
→ Independent
→ Persistent
→ Motivated
→ Interested in the unfamiliar, the mysterious, and the complex
→ Free from fear of criticism
→ A problem solver
→ Unstoppable
→ Brave
→ Intuitive
→ Trusting
→ Centered
→ Committed

- → In the flow
- → Following a calling
- → Playful
- → Joyful
- → Fun
- → Courageous
- → Relational
- → Questioning
- → Challenging
- → Attentive

Team Members' Phrases When They Are Succeeding at Being Creative

- ➜ I love this work!
- ➜ We are lucky to work here!
- ➜ We are lucky to have you on our team!
- ➜ We value your contributions!
- ➜ Do I have to go home?
- ➜ Life is great! Work is better!
- ➜ We are truly making a difference!
- ➜ I never dreamed that we could come up with such great ideas!
- ➜ Wild is good! Wacky is better!
- ➜ What a joy to create!
- ➜ I love that I don't have to leave half of myself at home.
- ➜ They really value all of me here.
- ➜ My sense of a calling is really being honored.
- ➜ I am doing something that matters.
- ➜ I really matter here!

→ I love being in the flow and watching the same in my teammates.

→ We are on a roll!

→ We did it! And we are going to keep on doing it!

→ We are celebrating tonight!

→ The best ideas come from knowing and hearing what matters most to each team member.

→ We have a terrific group of people to work with.

→ Being part of this creative team rocks!

→ It's unbelievable how many great ideas come out of our innovation meetings.

→ We do best when we trust the creative process.

→ We may feel uncomfortable while we're in the process, but that's okay. We will come out on the other side!

→ This team is great! We will do this!

→ I love the confidence we all have in one another.

→ We are going to lead the way with innovative ideas.

→ Our company is thinking well into the future.

Companies That Support Creative Teams

In *The Creative Spirit*, Daniel Goleman, Paul Kaufman, and Michael Ray offer the following examples of companies that changed the psychology of their workplaces so that employees felt confident enough to express their ideas freely.

The Body Shop

Anita Roddick, president of The Body Shop, which sells its own line of natural cosmetics developed without animal testing, was inspired by Third World cultures and the Quakers, who looked after employees, provided houses, built towns, were honorable, didn't tell lies, and valued labor. She modeled and developed a culture of:

- Telling the truth, with no fudging.
- Breaking the rules.
- Saying you're in love with the anarchist.
- Being open to suggestions.
- Surprising your people (for example, she asks, "What really ticks you off about us?" when meeting with staff members around the world in order to get to what works well and what doesn't).
- Refusing a rhetoric that says you'll listen and do nothing.
- Believing that a company can be run in a moral way.
- Making money, but also enhancing the spirituality of the workplace.
- Giving people the freedom to play and to take risks (for example, she closes the research and development labs on Friday afternoon—but anyone who wants to play around making products can go in).
- Running the company on feminine principles where the major ethic is care.
- Doing what looks risky to others when your convictions tell you it is right.
- Being a values-led entrepreneur.
- Making the environment a stimulating visual and sensory experience:
  - ❑ Hanging posters, charts, and photos that celebrate the human spirit by offering great thoughts and great images.
  - ❑ Using different displays, sounds, and things that people can physically touch so as to keep the senses alive.

- ❏ Changing the environment regularly, so that people fall in love with change.
- ❏ If *you're* bored going into the workspace, customers will be bored with the product as well.
- ■ Wanting success to be measured by more than financial yardsticks, including how good the company is to its employees and how it benefits the community.

Patagonia

Yvon Chouinard founded Patagonia, one of the most innovative sportswear companies in the world, because of his passion for mountain climbing and his need for good equipment. He started at 18 years old by designing and making his own piton. He:

- ■ Decided to do it on his own terms, breaking the rules.
- ■ Doesn't compete head on with other companies in his industry, but instead makes products that are noncompetitive.
- ■ Puts money into a very strong R&D department so as to have unique products, develops products quickly, and then drops them and goes in a different direction when everyone copies them.
- ■ Developed a company without a hierarchy or secrets, in which power is dispersed, everyone shares responsibility, and personal growth and independent initiative are encouraged.
- ■ Believes that the role of management is to instigate change, to throw down the gauntlet of a problem, and to expect everybody to work together imaginatively to figure out a solution.
- ■ Offers daycare on the premises so that parents can go back and forth and connect with their children. Then they won't

worry so much about their children and will feel more like they are at home.

■ Still works in the blacksmith's shop to clear his mind.

Skaltek

Öystein Skalleberg founded Skaltek, which designs, manufactures, and sells the heavy machinery used by the wire and cable industry. He disliked work in traditional companies, so he quit and founded his own, in which:

■ There are no cookie-cutter job descriptions.

■ Anyone might be involved in any number of functions, depending on need and desire.

■ Everyone is treated like an artist. ("Every human being is a Leonardo da Vinci.")

■ Each individual is her or his own quality controller, is given responsibility, and as a result develops a moral conscience about the work.

■ Everyone accompanies the delivery of the machines that she or he has designed and built, and trains those who will use the machines.

■ There are no traditional titles on business cards—everyone's title is "responsible person," and that's what it says on all the cards.

■ Weekly meetings of all employees include full disclosure of finances and salaries so that everyone knows what things cost and what the exact flow of money is for the week.

■ All employees are involved in setting salaries.

■ Everything is open to discussion by everyone.

AMEX Life Assurance

Sarah Nolan took over AMEX Life Assurance, an insurance company that was responding sluggishly to customer needs. She selected five managers from various parts of the business and put them in an office outside of the main building. She charged them with reinventing one division of the organization. "It's staggering how far people will go if they own the results," said Nolan. They increased profits for the division 700 percent by:

- Creating an open office design.
- Cutting levels of hierarchy from ten to three.
- Putting a computer on every desk.
- Welcoming innovative ideas.
- Erasing rigid job descriptions and expanding individual responsibility so that everyone was prepared to do every task.

SAS

Jan Carlzon of SAS ensured that:

- Many people share decision making, not just a few at the top of the pyramid.
- Customers are at the top of the organizational chart.
- Those who work with the customers are next on the organizational chart.
- Employees have the freedom, the responsibility, and the authority to make decisions on behalf of the company.
- The administration is at the bottom of the organizational chart, offering support to the "troops" who are on the front line.

- All the employees know that they are to use their intuition and feelings, not merely to conduct research and gather information.
- There are activities to lift people's spirits, like string quartets playing at lunch hour.
- Leaders are like fathers or coaches, interacting with the employees with respect, faith, and love so that they can dare to take risks, use their intuition, and achieve their full potential.

CHAPTER 3

A Structure for Creativity

Idea Management and Implementation

U p to this point, *Perfect Phrases for Creativity and Innovation* has aimed at instigating creative ideas and increasing creativity in the workplace in the pursuit of goals such as transforming organizations, increasing market share, or creating new products or product lines. Sometimes innovation is built into the DNA of a company, and creativity-enhancing strategies infuse the organizational structure and day-to-day activities (a condition that I would certainly echo Tom Peters in recommending). At other times, creativity is motivated by a problem or a crisis. This chapter identifies steps for problem solving and perfect phrases for including creativity in each step. These implementation steps may be used whenever innovation is deemed necessary for change initiatives. In general, the steps necessary for solving problems creatively include:

- **Selecting the creativity team** based on diverse interests, talents, and investment.
- **Defining the problem(s)** or the challenge(s) that is (are) facing the organization or company.
- **Generating or discovering potential solutions** to that (those) problem(s) or challenge(s).
- **Allowing for incubation of ideas.** (You may need to repeat this step periodically.)
- **Evaluating, prioritizing, and choosing** among the solutions identified.
- **Improving the solutions** based on the evaluation.
- **Generating a menu of potential strategies** to actualize the solutions.
- **Deciding on a step-by-step action plan** with a timeline and responsibilities.
- **Communicating the action plan** to key stakeholders in ways that increase their motivation to participate in or support the plan.
- **Implementing the action plan.**
- **Evaluating the results.**

Creativity or innovation strategies may be useful as part of several of these steps so as to generate as many ideas as possible. But following idea *generation*, individuals or teams need to *evaluate* the ideas and *choose* those that they will then *act* on. At each problem-solving step, then, individuals or teams:

- First, use various activities to stimulate *divergent* or *right-brain thinking* so as to generate as many ideas as possible. (More on these activities in the next chapter.)
- Then, use *convergent* or *left-brain thinking* to:
  - ❑ **Group** like ideas together into categories.
  - ❑ **Prioritize** the categories.

- ❑ **Develop criteria** for judging the ideas.
- ❑ **Use intuition and judgment** to select a category to act on or carry out.
- ❑ **Get feedback** on the best ideas.

Generating many ideas requires divergent thinking or right-brain activity. Categorization, prioritization, and selection of the change initiatives or actions to pursue require convergence, or left-brain activity. Action and communication plans, also converging strategies, should then target the highest-priority categories.

If problem solving, communication, and action planning are to be successful, Edward de Bono, in *Six Thinking Hats*, indicates the need to hear from people with all sorts of different perspectives. He categorizes these people or perspectives by color:

Blue Hat people remember the big picture or vision. It is often wise to hear Blue Hat perspectives at the beginning and end of a creativity meeting.

White Hat people remind teams of the essential facts, distinguishing them from beliefs or biases.

Green Hat people are able to generate many uncensored thoughts, which is very helpful during brainstorming or other divergent thinking processes.

Red Hat people tune in to the emotions surrounding the problems or solutions under consideration—their own, their team's, and those of anyone else who is likely to be affected by the problem or solution.

Black Hat people bring up the negatives, the objections, giving the team the opportunity to consider how to create alternatives and mitigations.

Yellow Hat people focus on the positives, the benefits, the opportunities, and the selling points when weighing the problem and its possible solutions.

Labeling people by hat color, or even inviting participants to wear the hats, communicates the value of each perspective in creating the best solutions. The hats give team members a shorthand for communicating which "hats" they need to hear more from and which they need to hear less from. Using the hats metaphor reduces blame and polarization among people who have a tendency to wear one particular hat more frequently than other hats.

Selecting the Creativity Team

Many phrases for selecting the creativity team are spread through the preceding chapters, so only a few are repeated here as reminders. The key to ensuring a highly creative team is to select a team of diverse people—people of different ages, passions, fields, cultures, experiences, departments, and skills—because, as stated in Chapter 1, the encounter with difference challenges each of us to leave the rut of the known and branch out into the unknown—and that's where creativity lives! Furthermore, a team needs to include people who demonstrate the characteristics described in Chapter 1, those who:

- Believe answers exist.
- Are open to people and ideas and are active explorers of the world around them.
- Value themselves.
- Experience a sense of "calling" in their work.

- Bring their right and left brains and their "child" to the creativity discussions.
- Trust the creativity process.
- Have developed expertise in their particular fields.

(Of course, hiring people who have these characteristics or developing and rewarding those who demonstrate such characteristics is also a good idea.) Finally, the creativity team needs an idea recorder and a leader with great facilitation skills, who can stay focused on the challenge.

Perfect Phrases for Selecting the Creativity Team

→ Let's make sure to include people who never agree with us.
→ We need to consider how we might ensure that we hear as many conflicting views as possible during our innovation meeting.
→ Let's create a team of people who don't tend to agree with one another to make sure we hear different perspectives.
→ We need to include people who have ideas that we might borrow and build on.
→ Creative use of others' ideas is just as important as generating our own.
→ Let's make a list of everyone who is involved in this problem.
→ Let's consider who else has had a similar problem and would have needed to come up with answers that we might find beneficial.
→ We need to ensure that we meet with people who have as many different perspectives as possible.

→ Let's consider whom we should include on our team so as to have as much diversity in culture, skills, opinions, talents, interests, and experiences as possible.

→ Let's spend a little time really listening to the people around us. Let's see whom we might want to hear more from.

→ I know you have talents that we will benefit from.

→ I want us to consider what expertise we need at this meeting to ensure that we are coming up with the best answers.

→ Let's include representatives from each of our different departments.

→ Let's ensure that we have included people from each of the professions represented in our organization.

→ We have lots of introverts in our department—let's ensure that we include some extraverts in our creativity meetings.

→ We need a diverse enough group that a variety of different views are represented.

→ We will need one of the researchers, one of the marketing people, and the head of finance to participate in this discussion.

→ Jerry has been here forever, so let's include him. But let's also include Sarah, the intern, Janica, one of our newer administrators, and Javier, the newest professional.

→ We need representatives on the team who have different kinds of information, different goals, different roles, and different experiences.

Defining the Problem

"Problem definition" is often given short shrift by those who are anxious to take action and to get problems solved. Unfortunately, taking action without fully understanding the problem can lead to investing an incredible amount of energy in solving, well, the wrong problem. So, as Goleman, Kaufman, and Ray advocate, we need to immerse ourselves in the problem, searching out anything that might be vaguely relevant to it, being open and receptive, and listening carefully. Defining the problem means deciding on:

- The job to be done
- The desired outcomes
- The purpose for which customers buy products and services

Two types of problems particularly warrant creative energy, according to David Silverstein, Philip Samuel, and Neil DeCarlo, authors of *The Innovator's Toolkit*: situations in which the problem is well defined, but better solutions are needed, and situations in which the problem is fuzzy, but plenty of solutions are available (for example, finding new applications for existing technologies).

Perfect Phrases for Defining the Problem

In the process of defining the problem, the team needs to ask:

→ What is the business or organization about? What are its:
  → Products?
  → Technologies?
  → Markets?
  → Functions?
  → Services?
→ What is the root cause of the problem?
→ What are all the other problems surrounding the chosen problem?

Michael Michalko and Jack Foster further suggest that *individuals* ask themselves the following questions in order to define the problem:

→ What do I wish would happen in my job?
→ What are my unfulfilled goals?
→ What excites me in my work?
→ What would I like to have or to accomplish?
→ What business idea would I like to work on?
→ What do I wish I had more time to do?
→ What more would I like to get out of my job?
→ What business relationship would I like to improve?
→ What would I like to do better?
→ What have I complained about?
→ What changes for the worse do I see in the attitudes of others?
→ What angers me at my work?
→ What misunderstandings do I have at work?
→ What takes too long?
→ What is too complicated?
→ What would I like to get others to do?
→ What would I like to organize better?
→ In what ways could I make more money at work?
→ What changes would I like to introduce?
→ What is wasted?
→ What wears me out?
→ What in my job turns me off?
→ Where are the bottlenecks?
→ In what ways am I inefficient?
→ What are all the things that bug me?

Michael Michalko suggests that *teams* might ask themselves additional questions when defining problems or identifying business challenges:

→ What creative suggestions can we make about new product ideas?

→ How can we better differentiate our product from all others?

→ How can we cut costs and increase production?

→ How can we become indispensable to the company?

→ How can we sell 20 percent more than we are selling at present?

→ What new product(s) is (are) needed? What extension of a current product's market could there be?

→ How can we better handle customer complaints?

→ What new selling techniques can we create?

→ Can we reduce the cost of our current selling techniques?

→ Is it possible to encourage everyone in our organization to actively look for ways to better differentiate our products?

→ How can we improve the role that service plays in the sale of our products?

→ How can we become more customer-oriented?

→ Is it possible to change our corporate image?

→ How can our advertising better communicate the benefits of our goods and services?

→ What awards would be more meaningful to employees?

→ What procedures could we institute that would reduce unnecessary paperwork?

→ In what ways might we outperform the competition?

→ Which of our products can we make into silver bullets (leading products or services in a particular industry)?

Then, Jack Foster and Michael Michalko suggest that *teams* might ask themselves the following questions to further refine their understanding of the problem:

→ Why is it necessary to solve the problem?
→ What benefits will we gain by solving the problem?
→ What isn't the problem?
→ What is unknown?
→ What information do we have?
→ What is it that we don't yet understand?
→ Is the information sufficient? Or is it insufficient, redundant, or contradictory?
→ Where are the boundaries of the problem?
→ Let's list as many problems as we can, anything that is hindering us from reaching our goals.
→ Can we separate the various parts of the problem? Can we write them down? What are the relationships among the parts of the problem?
→ Should we draw a diagram or a figure of the problem?
→ What are the constants of the problem (things that can't be changed)?
→ Have we seen the problem before?
→ Do we know of a related problem?
→ What if we try to think of a familiar problem that has the same or a similar unknown?
→ Can we restate our problem? How many different ways can we restate it? Can we make it more general or more specific? Can the rules be changed?
→ Have we seen this problem in a slightly different form?
→ Suppose we find a problem related to ours that has already been solved. Can we use the solution? Can we use its method?

→ What are the best, worst, and most probable cases we can imagine?
→ What are our major goals?
→ What is getting in the way of those goals?
→ What would we like to achieve?
→ Let's list everything we would like to achieve and why.
→ If we could fix anything we wanted to, how would we do it?
→ Let's get clear on what matters to us.
→ What is currently hindering us from achieving it?
→ If we had all the money in the world, what would we do differently?
→ If we could snap our fingers and make our situation better, what would we do?

Next, according to Jack Foster, *teams* need to investigate the problem thoroughly by asking the following questions:

→ How long has the problem existed?
→ When didn't it exist?
→ What results from the problem?
→ Why does it occur?
→ In what current circumstances doesn't it exist?
→ Who's involved?
→ Who isn't involved?
→ What are its parameters (size, color, weight, and so on)?
→ What does it influence?
→ What causes it?
→ What influences it?
→ What additional problems does it cause?
→ What makes it hard to overcome?
→ Who wants to overcome it?
→ Who doesn't?

→ Let's name the characteristics of our problem, then see what else has those characteristics and what might we learn from that other thing.

In searching for the answers to these questions, Foster suggests that *leaders* might ask *team members* to:

→ "Masticate" everything they have found out about the problem and the facts surrounding it.
→ Keep their minds on the problem.
→ Become investigators into every detail.
→ Become possessed.
→ Read books.
→ Read articles.
→ Drill deep.
→ Read the newspaper.
→ Read a blog.
→ Visit the plant.
→ Visit the warehouse.
→ Search the Internet.
→ Become more like a child and ask questions.
→ Talk with the workers.
→ Ask why.
→ Ask why not.
→ Talk with the suppliers.
→ Seek out customers and talk with them.
→ Seek out noncustomers and talk with them.
→ Work in the store.
→ Ride with the salespeople.
→ Sample the product.
→ Sample competitors' products.
→ Go to the library.

→ Go to bookstores.
→ Talk with the engineers.
→ Talk with the designers.
→ Seek out competitors' customers and talk with them.
→ Read competitors' annual reports.
→ Work on the truck.
→ Work in the field.
→ Go to lectures.
→ Ask their kids.
→ Ask their friends.
→ Ask their mothers.

Exercises to Further Focus Problem Definition

Is/Is Not

Once teams have decided on a problem focus, Hemsley Fraser, a global training company, suggests that the *Is/Is Not* exercise can help them to:

→ Discover any assumptions that are being made about the issue.
→ Break the issue down into manageable parts that enable action to be taken.
→ Clear up ambiguous language.
→ Help a group to align around common definitions or perceptions of the problem.

Conduct the exercise by saying to the group:

→ Write the problem at the top of a flipchart.
→ Create two columns headed by the titles "Is" and "Is Not."
→ Brainstorm as many ideas as possible about what the problem is or is not.

→ Consider possible relationships between what is written on the two sides of the chart.

Five Whys

Taiichi Ohno suggests that the *Five Whys* can help teams discover the root cause of problems.

→ Ask the first "why" question: "Why does Problem X exist?"
→ Then, ask a second "why" question based on the answer to the first "why" question: "Okay, but why did that occur?"
→ Keep challenging each response with a new question until you reach a root cause and can go no further.
→ Then ask the group: "How has this exercise helped you to understand the problem?"

Jump Back

Hemsley Fraser uses this exercise to help people "jump back" from drawing conclusions too soon about a problem. Teams ask themselves:

→ What conclusion have I already reached?
→ Stepping back from that conclusion, how did I interpret the situation?
→ Stepping back again, what experiences, beliefs, or assumptions led me to that interpretation?
→ Stepping back once more, what happened to trigger those beliefs or assumptions?
→ Stepping back from those triggers, can I describe only the facts in a neutral way?
→ Could those facts and data be interpreted in other ways?
→ How willing or able am I to challenge and rethink my original conclusion?

→ What have I discovered about the problem as a result of "jumping back" multiple times?

Problem Tree

The Department of Energy uses a *Risk Tree* or *Problem Tree* to better understand an issue. The Problem Tree helps creativity teams explore a problem's root causes and anticipate its potential impacts and consequences. Many different diagrams for the Problem Tree are available online to facilitate thinking about root causes and effects of a particular problem. Figure 3.1 shows one option.

Pointing to the diagram, say:

→ Write the risk or problem in the center of the diagram or on the "trunk" of the tree.

→ Brainstorm all possible causes of the risk or problem that you can think of and write them on sticky notes that you then place below the trunk.

→ Group the problem's causes into clusters that are related, and connect primary causes with any contributing causes.

→ Place the contributing causes below the primary causes, and connect them to the relevant primary causes.

→ Now do the same for consequences, which become the branches above the focal risk or problem, placing primary consequences on the largest branches and secondary consequences on smaller branches.

→ What has the diagram helped you to understand about the problem?

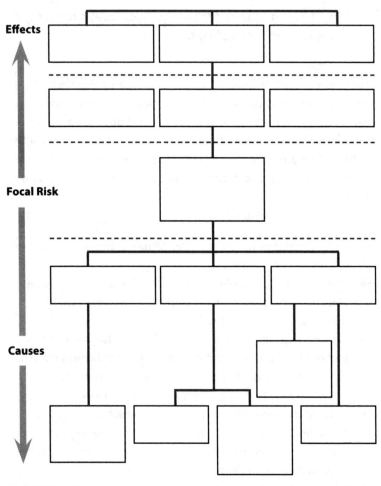

Figure 3.1

Challenge Statements

After the team members have used these *divergent* questions and strategies in analyzing the problem, and have gathered as much information on the problem as they can, Hemsley Fraser suggests that they use *convergent* thinking to:

- Clarify their understanding if needed. Leaders might ask:
  - ❑ Does everyone understand the problem(s)?
  - ❑ Is further explanation needed on the problem(s)?
- Select the most urgent problems to work on—those whose solution will do the most good and those that most need consideration—and mark them. Leaders might say:
  - ❑ Gather around the flipchart(s) and consider which problems seem important to work on first.
  - ❑ Use green sticky dots for the problems that seem the most urgent.
  - ❑ Use blue dots for problems whose solutions will do the most good.
  - ❑ Use yellow dots for problems that you believe need consideration at some point.
- Cluster the "hits" that relate to each other.
- Name each cluster.
- Create a hierarchy of problems in the order in which they ought to be addressed. Leaders might ask:
  - ❑ Which of these problems seem more important to address first?
  - ❑ Which problems are more feasible to address?
  - ❑ How are these problems related to one another?
  - ❑ How might we visually picture the relationships among problems?
  - ❑ Which problems are connected with others? How?
- Finally, leaders might ask teams to select the cluster that stands out most for them or combine several clusters to focus the needed work.

This process eventually culminates in what Hemsley Fraser calls a Challenge Statement. A Challenge Statement is a future-focused, open question that emphasizes the *desired outcome* or overall goal. It ensures focus on the core issue and facilitates communication with others about the issue.

Perfect Phrases for Challenge Statements

A Challenge Statement is one or two sentences that:
- → Begin with a statement like:
    - → It would be great if . . .
    - → I wish we could . . .
    - → How might we . . .
- → And include a general overview of:
    - → What needs to be accomplished
    - → Any criteria or requirements for how it will be accomplished
    - → The result or outcome when it is accomplished

An example of a Challenge Statement might be: "It would be great if we could transform our organizational culture and work processes in a way that leverages innovative technology and workforce talent to maximize patient satisfaction, optimize employee functioning and joy at work, and meet patient care needs in the shortest time possible."

Generating Solutions

Most of the phrases presented up to this point in *Perfect Phrases for Creativity and Innovation* help individuals and teams to generate or discover creative solutions to problems, so these phrases will not be repeated here. In addition, the chapters following also include many activities that are designed to stimulate the development of vast quantities of ideas through triggering divergent, right-brain thought and assisting people in bringing all of themselves to the creativity table. In order to encourage team members to think about potential solutions or to prepare before meeting together, team leaders or facilitators might send everyone an agenda in advance. Participants might also be required to bring a certain number of ideas as their entrance ticket to the meeting. Of key importance in generating many ideas about potential solutions to the problem is separating the right-brain, idea-generation step from the left-brain, evaluating, prioritizing, and choosing activities. If individuals or teams jump too quickly to left-brain activities, creativity will sag.

Perfect Phrases for Generating Solutions

Michael Michalko suggests asking the following questions in the process of generating solutions:

→ What is the unique set of qualities that makes this problem what it is?
→ Can you solve the whole problem? Part of the problem?

→ What would you like the resolution to be? Can you picture a resolution?

→ How much of the unknown can you determine?

→ Have you taken all essential notions in the problems into account?

→ Can you derive something useful from the information you have?

→ Have you used all of the information you have?

→ Can you see the result? How many different kinds of results can you see?

→ What creative-thinking techniques can you use to generate ideas? How many different techniques might you use?

→ Can you arrive at solutions intuitively? How might you check the result?

→ Can you separate the steps in the problem-solving process?

→ Can you determine the correctness of each step?

→ How many different ways have you tried to solve the problem?

→ What have others done to solve the problem?

→ What do you think should be done?

→ What do you need to do at this time?

→ How should it be done?

→ Who should do it?

→ Where should it be done?

→ Who will be responsible for what?

→ When should it be done?

→ Can you use this problem as information for solving some other problem?

→ What milestones might best mark your progress?

→ How will you know when you're successful?

If, however, individuals or teams have generated a great number of ideas without latching on to "the big one"—the one that seems as though it will create the most transformative change—they may find themselves frustrated, searching laboriously for the best solution, struggling to agree on the best solutions, digging deeper and deeper holes, and experiencing what Goleman, Kaufman, and Ray call a "darkness before the dawn." Because brain connections become stronger with repetition, David Murray believes it may be hard to get out of the usual pathways or grooves in our thinking. It is then time to allow ideas to incubate.

Incubating Ideas

Incubation strategies might include activities such as:

- Purposely taking a break
- Taking an intellectual vacation
- Sleeping on it
- Shifting gears
- Taking a creative pause
- Clearing out thoughts to make space for new ones
- Changing activities in order to allow the problem and possible solutions to simmer in the unconscious
- Intentionally engaging in "conversation" with our shadow self
- Focusing on opposites
- Letting the subconscious mind take over
- Relaxing the watchman
- Bringing other parts of ourselves to bear on the ideas

At some point, as we focus on something other than the problem at hand, when we are listening to our feelings or our Freudian slips, illumination dawns. "Suddenly the answer comes, as if from nowhere," say Goleman, Kaufman, and Ray. The "majority of cognitive psychologists agree that the brain is able to accomplish higher-order processing [and come up with better solutions] without conscious awareness," says James Adams, author of *The Care and Feeding of Ideas*.

Perfect Phrases for Incubating Ideas

Individuals or teams might use the following phrases to encourage people to let ideas incubate:

→ Let's take some time and sleep on it.
→ We have been working hard to develop ideas; let's let them percolate for a while.
→ We really need to take a break and do something else. I have stopped making any forward progress.
→ I'd like everyone to stop the intentional problem solving or strategizing and do something very different—for example:
  → Exercise.
  → Sing in the shower.
  → Daydream.
  → Relax.
  → Laugh.
  → Be playful.
  → Take a long drive.
  → Create art.
  → Play with your children.
  → Walk by the ocean.
  → Enjoy the autumn leaves.
  → Go to church.

- → Sing in the choir.
- → Move your body and focus on its movements.
- → Take a quiet walk.
- → Do yoga.
- → Sleep.
- → Make love.
- → Eat chocolate.
- → Go shopping.
- → Clean the house.
- → Take a swim.
- → Ride your bike.
- → Walk in the park.
- → Watch television.
- → Play a game.
- → Go out to dinner.
- → Read a good book.
- → Talk with your spouse.
- → Draw a picture.
- → Plan your vacation.
- → Sew a costume.
- → Create some pottery.
- → Visit the neighbors.
- → Mow the lawn.
- → Pull some weeds.
- → Plant some flowers.
- → Search for that stereo you want.
- → Plan a party.
- → Read a funny blog.

→ What is your gut telling you?
→ Pay attention to your intuition.
→ Consider your hunches.
→ What does your instinct tell you?

➜ We will reconvene tomorrow (or next week) and see what has emerged during incubation.

Solution Statements

By the time individuals or teams have generated ideas and allowed them to incubate, they will have filled many flipcharts with ideas. But acting on all these ideas would be impossible. So, choosing which ideas to focus and build on comes next. And choosing a solution or solutions requires its own *convergent* process—grouping ideas, identifying the best ideas, and prioritizing the ideas based on feasibility and potential. The following tools with their perfect phrases might be helpful in doing so. Individuals or teams write ideas on sticky notes before putting them on flipcharts so that they can be moved around, grouped, and put in priority order.

Perfect Phrases for Clarifying Understanding and Grouping Ideas

Clarify understanding if needed, asking:

➜ Does everyone understand the solutions that are being proposed?
➜ Are further explanations needed on any of them?

Use different-colored sticky dots to evaluate preferred choices. You might say,

➜ Use green dots for the ideas that are most promising.
➜ Use blue dots for ideas that are intriguing.

→ Use yellow dots for ideas that you would like to consider at some point.

Group individual ideas into categories and name the categories. You might say,

→ Now that you have evaluated which ideas you like best, consider which of those ideas might be similar, might belong together, or might be connected in some way. Group these together.

→ [After they have grouped them] Now give each grouping a name that best represents its ideas or actions.

Perfect Phrases for Determining Criteria and Prioritizing Ideas

Determine the criteria by which you want to prioritize the ideas. Leaders might say:

→ What criteria do we want to use to make our decisions?
→ Are we interested in feasibility, cost, or timing?
→ What is most important to us in making these choices?

Prioritize the categories or groups. Consider or ask the team to consider:

→ Which categories does it make sense to focus on first, next, and so on?
→ Which categories are most feasible (costs less or are easiest to implement)?

→ Which are less risky (based on costs and the likelihood of success)?
→ Which offer the promise of the most positive outcomes?
→ Which offer our company the most competitive edge?
→ Which offer the most value-added?
→ Which solve the most problems?

Finally, select the category that stands out or combine several clusters in order to focus the needed work.

This process eventually culminates in a Solution Statement in response to the Challenge Statement that was developed earlier. According to Hemsley Fraser, the Solution Statement is:

■ A future-focused statement of what will be.
■ An overall description of what the team will do to address the problem.

The statement begins with "What we see ourselves doing is. . . ."

Perfect Phrases for Solution Statements

In response to the Challenge Statement suggested earlier ("It would be great if we could transform our organizational culture and work processes in a way that leverages innovative technology and workforce talent to maximize patient satisfaction, optimizes employee functioning and joy at work, and meets patient care needs in the shortest time possible."), a Solution Statement might be:

What we see ourselves doing is:

→ Improving relationships and communication among people and sites.

→ Educating people about new IT platforms that can improve services and flexibility.

→ Improving staff capabilities and joy through training, coaching, and regular "success lunches," in which staff members hear what others are doing.

→ Surveying patients to determine areas for improving satisfaction.

Evaluating Solutions

A variety of tools may be helpful in thinking critically about the solutions that have been generated, in order to evaluate the top choices. Some possible tools are suggested here, along with procedures and perfect phrases that can help leaders or facilitators aim their teams in helpful directions.

Pluses/Potential/Concerns (or Cost/Benefit Analysis)

In this activity, participants become clearer about the value of potential solutions, as well as potential concerns.

Perfect Phrases for Pluses/Potential/ Concerns (or Cost/Benefit Analysis)

After explaining the purpose of the exercise, leaders might say (allowing participants to work in response to each phrase before moving on to the next):

→ Using divergent thinking, list as many positives about the solution as you can, as quickly as possible.

→ Now list as many potential positive spin-offs (potentials) as you can think of that could occur if we choose this solution.

→ Next, continuing to use divergent thinking, list as many concerns as you can about the potential solution. Don't forget to move quickly and to think of as many wild and crazy ideas as you can.

→ List the top three of each: pluses, potentials, and concerns. (Note that this is convergent thinking.)

→ After reviewing each, again use divergent thinking to generate ideas about how to respond to each of the top concerns.

→ Using all of the pluses, potentials, concerns, and possible resolutions to the concerns that have been discussed, decide how to improve your Solution Statement in a way that takes what you have discovered into consideration.

Risk Map

After team members have conducted an activity similar to Pluses/Potential/Concerns, in which they have identified their top concerns about potential solutions, Hemsley Fraser suggests using a Risk Map to assist in evaluating the risks of the solutions under consideration. For each of the concerns identified, participants rate the probability of the risk or concern occurring and the significance of the risk or concern if it did occur, using a scale from 1 to 5, with 1 being least likely or least significant and 5 being most likely or most significant.

They then map the risks on the Risk Map in order to visually understand whether they should terminate, track, treat (fix or attend to), or tolerate the risks.

Perfect Phrases for a Risk Map

After explaining the Risk Map's purpose, team leaders might say:

→ Next to the list of your concerns, indicate from 1 to 5, with 1 being the least and 5 being the most, the probability that what you are concerned about (that is, the risk) will occur.

→ Do the same to indicate how significant a problem it will be if what you are concerned about actually happens.

Team members might fill out a chart like the one in Figure 3.2.

Risk	Significance if It Occurs	Probability of Occurrence	Quadrant
Increased costs	3	2	Tolerate or track
Personnel upheaval	3	3	Center
Patient care disruption	5	3	Track or terminate

Figure 3.2

Team leaders then might say:

→ Next, plot the scores on the Risk Map, marking the points in the quadrant where the probability and the significance meet (see Figure 3.3).

→ After mapping the significance and probability of each risk, list what you will need to do in response to each risk—terminate it, track it without doing anything at this point, monitor and manage it (treat it), or tolerate it.

The actions to be taken on the risks in the chart in Figure 3.2 are noted in the fourth column of the chart.

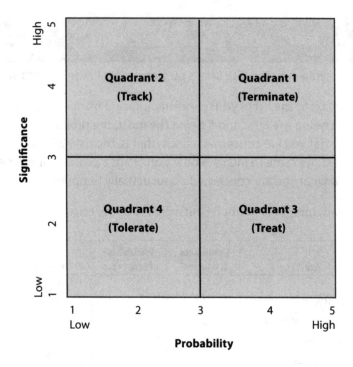

Figure 3.3   Risk Map

Opportunity Map

The Opportunity Map, according to Hemsley Fraser, assists people in evaluating the potential of the solutions they have been considering. After having identified solutions to one or more problems, participants rate each solution's (opportunity's) potential to benefit the organization, meet a need, or alleviate a problem on a scale from 1 to 5, with 1 indicating the least potential and 5 indicating the most potential. They next rate the solution's feasibility, or how easily or quickly it can be accomplished, on a scale from 1 to 5, with 1 being the least feasible and 5 being the most feasible.

They then map the solutions on an Opportunity Map in order to visually understand whether to seize, shelve, study, or skip that solution. The value of a solution or opportunity is a function of its feasibility combined with its potential.

Perfect Phrases for an Opportunity Map

After explaining the purpose of the Opportunity Map, team leaders might say:

➜ Next to the list of your solutions, indicate from 1 to 5, with 1 being least and 5 being most, the potential offered by the solution (that is, the opportunity) you are considering.
➜ Do the same to indicate how feasible the solution or opportunity is.

The participants might fill out a chart like the one in Figure 3.4.

Opportunity—Improved Communication	Potential	Feasibility	Quadrant
Pop-up upon turning on computer—change weekly	3	5	Seize or shelve
Use electronic bulletin boards—change weekly	4	5	Seize
Monthly newsletter with hidden puzzles and prizes for those who solve the puzzles	3	4	Seize or shelve

Figure 3.4

Team leaders might next say:

→ Next, plot the scores on the Opportunity Map, marking the points where the potential and feasibility meet (see Figure 3.5).

→ After mapping the potential and feasibility of each solution or opportunity, decide which of the opportunities you will seize because its potential and feasibility seem to warrant the most immediate implementation or consideration.

The actions to be taken on the opportunities in the Opportunity Chart in Figure 3.4 are noted in the fourth column of the chart.

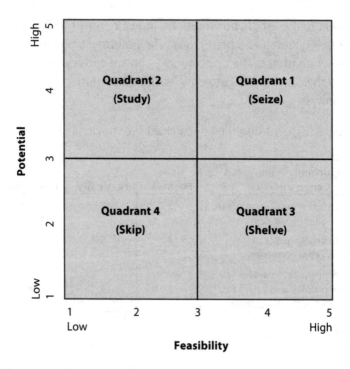

Figure 3.5   Opportunity Map

Murder Board

Michael Michalko suggests using a Murder Board to get feedback on ideas or solutions. The aim is to compare ideas, narrow the field, identify the strengths and weaknesses of ideas, receive suggestions on improvements and modifications, identify business opportunities for the ideas, clarify marketing opportunities and concerns, and determine the level of interest in the ideas. The steps are as follows:

- Share your idea(s) with a trusted friend or significant other who will tell you the truth.
- Detail the idea or proposal in writing, stating the goals, assumptions, concerns, needs for information, your beliefs, what inspired the idea, why you want feedback, what kind of feedback you want, and questions you need answered.
- Select a group of people to give you feedback in writing or in person.
- Ask the group to critique the ideas (commit "murder" on them if they can) as harshly as possible.

Perfect Phrases for a Murder Board

Questions that an individual (change the pronouns for a group idea) might ask the Murder Board include:

- → Is the idea communicated clearly and completely?
- → What do you think about the idea?
- → How unique is the idea, from your perspective?
- → Would you be interested in the idea?
- → Do you think I have the capacity to carry this idea through to fruition?

- ➔ Is there a need for this solution?
- ➔ Is the market right for this idea?
- ➔ What are the idea's competitive advantages?
- ➔ How would you market this idea?
- ➔ What markets would you target with the idea?
- ➔ Is this a good time for this idea?
- ➔ What might be a better time?
- ➔ Given what you know of me and my interests, strengths, and competencies, do you think it is a good idea for me to carry out?
- ➔ Have I considered the costs realistically and completely?
- ➔ How feasible is the idea? How feasible is my trying to carry out the idea?

Improving Solutions

After the significant effort spent in evaluating the initially proposed solutions, it is time to improve on the Solution Statement.

Perfect Phrases for Improving the Solutions

Team leaders might say:

- ➔ Now that we have carefully weighed our original solutions to the problem(s), let's revise our Solution Statement.
- ➔ How might we improve it?
- ➔ What might we add?
- ➔ What might we leave out?
- ➔ How might we alter the wording to clarify it?
- ➔ Who might we consult for other ideas?

When these questions have been addressed, and the Solution Statement improved, the Solution Statement provides a rallying point to gather around, a target toward which to aim activities over the next several months.

Strategies to Actualize the Solutions

As is probably apparent in the sample solution statement given earlier, actualizing the solution will require breaking it down into steps or substatements. For instance, in order to improve relationships and communication among people and sites, as is indicated in the previous solution statement, a team might decide to start a weekly newsletter, have regular "meet and greets," create working groups made up of people from different sites, or have key information pop up on people's computers as soon as they turn them on. Of course, the possibilities are endless and would depend on the people, the site, the industry, and many other factors. But at this point, divergent thinking is again needed to generate as many ideas as possible about how to accomplish the outcomes listed in the Solution Statement.

Perfect Phrases for Strategies to Actualize the Solutions

A leader might use any of the activities described in the next chapter to stimulate ideas, saying,

→ Let's come up with as many ideas as possible about:
  → How we might meet our goals
  → What steps we need to take
  → What would be the best way to accomplish what we want to accomplish

→ What strategies would be most effective in generating the outcomes we are looking for
→ What strategies need to come first, second, and third
→ What the timelines or "dates to accomplish" each step ought to be

As with any of the diverging experiences already discussed, the next step would be to converge by evaluating, categorizing, and prioritizing (please review the specific phrases given earlier)—that is:

- Use sticky dots to indicate which ideas are most and least promising, interesting, or doable.
- Categorize the most promising ideas and give the categories names.
- Prioritize the categories.

Communication Planning

Just because *we* have given a great deal of thought to our ideas and are ourselves energized and excited by their possibilities doesn't mean that *others* will automatically share our energy and excitement. Different people have different agendas and needs. Politics often rules the day. And so, if we want our ideas to come to fruition after all of the energy we have invested in developing them, we need to take each individual stakeholder or stakeholder group's needs, interests, and motivations into consideration. Publicity is a great way to usurp bureaucracy and authority. Publicity is sometimes necessary to teach people how a product can benefit them. Developing a Communication Plan in chart form, as many of the Hemsley Fraser trainings do, does just this.

Perfect Phrases for Communication Planning

First, we need to ask:

→ In relation to our initiative(s), who are the key decision makers, influencers, implementers, and others who will be affected or must be or will be involved? Who has a stake in the innovation we are proposing? [Make a list.]

→ What is each stakeholder's level of knowledge about the problem or our proposed solution(s)? [Rate each person or group on a scale of 1 to 5.]

→ What do these people care about?

→ What are each stakeholder's primary needs or concerns— that is, what does each stakeholder really care about? What are the various stakeholders working on currently? What are their goals? What are they invested in? What is their agenda?

→ What need of theirs might my answer address?

→ What possibilities does our innovation increase, and how might these benefit those whom I need to support my idea?

→ What do we want each stakeholder to do or say in order to facilitate our goals?

→ How can we put our initiative in language that stakeholders care about so as to motivate them to get involved?

→ How might we piggyback our initiative onto something that the stakeholders are already working on?

→ How might our successes help the stakeholders to accomplish something that they are invested in or care about?

→ What else do I need to consider in marketing my idea?

→ Who else do I need to bring in to market my idea or to get other people on board?

➜   How might I plan for resistance?
➜   Who might I bring onto my team to share the load and increase the persuasive appeal?

You might write out the answers to these questions in chart form, as in Figure 3.6.

If you run into resistance with any of the stakeholders, Hemsley Fraser suggests that you might:

■ Focus on areas of agreement: "So, one thing we know we agree on . . ."
■ Softly restate the differences: "It appears we have some differences in . . ."
■ Negotiate or make proposals: "What could you support . . .?" "What if we tried . . . ?"
■ Reflect feelings: "You seem concerned about . . ."
■ Use positive body language, like eye contact and leaning in.
■ Probe for specifics to clarify areas of agreement and disagreement.
■ Draw out all viewpoints: "You look like you have something to add here. . . ."
■ Ask for input on obstacles and ways to overcome them: "Can you tell me why you feel reluctant?" "What would we need to do to get you on board?"

Action Planning

If a team leaves a creativity meeting without having decided on an action plan, the chances of follow-through on creative ideas are reduced. After all, we are all busy, we have many things on our plates, and we need to set priorities. We may care a lot about the initiatives we have been discussing. But if we don't formalize an action plan, any needed action may slip to the back of the file or the desk or the mind. Teams that successfully implement their ideas ensure that they end meetings with a clear idea of who is going to do what and when. So, again, beginning with divergent thinking, you might say to your team:

- Write on a flipchart all of the ideas you have about what we need to do to get moving on this initiative.
- Let's ensure that we list everything that needs to be done this week first (short-term).
- Then let's list what comes next (medium-term and long-term).
- Let's decide who needs to be involved.
- I want to get clear on who will be responsible for what actions.
- We need to decide what actions need to come first (and next, and so on) because other actions depend on them.

After diverging, by putting many needed actions on a flipchart and discovering all of the people who need to take action, be consulted, or approve the actions, groups need to converge by creating either an Action Plan or a RASCI chart.

For the Action Plan, list all of the short-term, medium-term, and long-term actions that need to be taken in the second column. Then, in the third column, identify who will take responsibility for each of the actions in the second column, and indicate when the action needs to be completed in the fourth column. In the fifth column, list who else is or needs to be involved in this action; and in the sixth column, indicate the date when the actors will report back on their progress, whether at the next meeting or at some informal meeting or conversation before the next scheduled meeting. For the initiative being described here, Figure 3.7 shows what some entries in the Action Plan might be.

COMMUNICATION PLANNER

"Improving Communication among People and Sites"

Pop-ups, Electronic Bulletin Board, Newsletter with Puzzles, and Prizes

Stakeholders	Knowledge	Desired Action/Outcome	Primary Needs/Concerns	Key Points to Address
Decision Makers				
Director	1	Approve actions/ funds	Optimize patient care at lowest costs possible	Up-to-date information critical to patient care and reducing waste
CFO	1	Find funds	Optimize patient care at lowest costs possible	Up-to-date information critical to patient care and reducing waste
Influencers				
Department chairs	5	"Sell" to all others	All personnel knowing what they are supposed to do. Being up-to-date on current procedures	Initiators of solution, so don't need persuading
Supervisors	2	Persuade staff to create content	Having a means to inform their staff and stay informed themselves	An efficient, up-to-date way to stay informed and ensure that your staff has current information
Staff	1	Motivate others to create content	Staying informed so as to avoid mistakes and provide optimal care to patients	Have access to most up-to-date information so as to provide optimal patient care

Stakeholders	Knowledge	Desired Action/Outcome	Primary Needs/Concerns	Key Points to Address
Implementers				
IT	1	Create space online Upload content	Effective use of IT systems to optimize patient care	An opportunity to put IT front and center in optimizing patient care
Communications committee	1	Create and approve content	Up-to-date communications that all employees have access to and use effectively	An efficient, cost-effective way to ensure that the whole hospital has up-to-date information
Department chairs	5	Create content	All personnel knowing what they are supposed to do. Being up-to-date on current procedures	Initiators of solution, so don't need persuading
Supervisors	2	Create content	Having a means to inform their staff and stay informed themselves	An efficient, up-to-date way to stay informed and ensure that staff has current information
Staff	1	Create content	Staying informed so as to avoid mistakes and provide optimal care to patients	Have access to most up-to-date information so as to provide optimal patient care

Figure 3.6 *(continued)*

ACTION PLAN

	Action(s) Needed	Who Acts	By When	Who Else Involved	Report Time
Short-term	Create graphic portraying benefits	Team leader, Graphics Department	Next week	Feedback from team	Final to team at 1/12 meeting
Medium-term	Discuss proposal with director	Team meets with director	1/12 meeting	Team and director; whomever director invites	Review meeting immediately following
	Make improvements in graphic	Team leader, Graphics Department	1/31	Team offers feedback on e-mailed new graphic	1/31 meeting
Long-term	Use/distribute graphic via multiple vehicles (i.e., e-mail, web page, pop-ups, newsletter)	Team, Team leader, PR Department, IT Department, Graphics Department	Set dates for conversations with departments; Set dates for rollout based on conversations	Same as who acts plus director for approvals	2/14 TBD

Figure 3.7

The RASCI chart, proposed by Rose Hightower, offers another format for clearly articulating the actions to be taken and the people responsible. The following instructions assist group participants to create a RASCI chart:

- What is the project name?
- List in the left column the key steps, processes, tasks, or activities necessary to ensure completion of the project.
- List across the top of the columns the people who need to be involved to ensure that the project is completed successfully.
- Indicate the following for each task:
  - ❑ R = person responsible for successful completion of the task.
  - ❑ A = person to whom R answers for the work, from whom R must obtain approval, authorization, or sign-off.
  - ❑ S = people who can support the effort by providing needed resources or other assistance.
  - ❑ C = people who have specific information or skills that are needed to complete the work.
  - ❑ I = those people who need to be kept informed of the project's progress and results.

Figure 3.8 gives an example of a completed RASCI chart for a proposed marketing effort.

Who? → ↓ What?	Regional Manager	Customer Care	Legal Department	Communications	Finance/ Accounting	Purchasing/ Fulfillment
Gather/review/ summarize branch experience reports	R	C		S		
Conduct focus groups	S	R		A/C	A	
Produce sample print materials	A		A	R		I
Develop media plan	I			R	A	I
Create cost projections	I			R	A/C	C
Write/produce final proposal	A	S		C		

Figure 3.8   RASCI Chart

Perfect Phrases for Implementing the Action Plan

Decisions and plans are critical and should not be given short shrift. However, they serve no purpose if people don't actually act on them. Leaders, managers, and supervisors, therefore, need to track progress on projects, and need to offer encouragement, inspiration, or other forms of motivation to keep their people moving on the action plans they have created. For instance, they might say to those responsible:

→ How are you doing on _____ ?

→ I would like to hear about your progress so far on _____ .

→ How far along are you?

→ Let's talk about how well we are meeting our targets.

→ What is working well and/or what additional support might you need in completing your part of the project?

→ I would like to review progress to this point.

→ What have you discovered as you have worked on this? Anything that affects the original plans?

→ Let's consider what adjustments in the plans or target dates may be necessary.

→ How can I help you to be successful?

→ What do we need to do to ensure that your part of the project is completed by the target date?

→ Please keep me updated on your progress.

→ Send me an e-mail each time you reach a target.

→ We are a little behind on our targets. What do we need to do to catch up? What is hindering our success? What can I do to help remove any hindrances?

Perfect Phrases for Increasing the Chances for Successful Change Efforts

John Kotter, in *Winning at Change*, indicates that "fewer than 15 of the 100 or more companies I have studied have successfully transformed themselves." This is disheartening, to say the least. It is particularly disheartening when we consider the amount of money, time, and effort spent by companies and by consultants, trainers, and others who are supposed to be experts in organizational transformation. Kotter uses this research result to launch his argument in *The Heart of Change* that eight "change levers" are necessary if change initiatives are to succeed. His argument is very persuasive that those who are implementing creative solutions need to consider how to:

→ Increase the urgency for change with quick, pointed, emotional appeals.
→ Build a guiding team that has power, status, expertise, and commitment.
→ Communicate the vision so as to get understanding and buy-in.
→ Create a change vision and strategy that you communicate and model regularly.
→ Empower action and remove obstacles by carefully choosing people and developing structures.
→ Create short-term wins with early surefire projects and rewards.
→ Build momentum by continuously improving the effort along the way.
→ Build a supportive culture with success stories, rewards, and new hires who understand the organization's values.

Those who are initiating organizational transformation efforts clearly need to come up to speed on how to actualize this advice in their own situations.

Evaluating Results

When problems are defined and solutions proposed, organizations clearly expect to meet certain goals in solving the problems. These goals are articulated in the Solution Statement, but metrics may need to be established to allow organizations to determine accurately whether the goals have been met and to what degree.

Perfect Phrases for Evaluating the Results

Some metrics may include formalized evaluation tools (such as 360-degree evaluations or a Trust Survey). In other cases, goal statements might state target dates and include such phrases as:

→ We will increase:
- → Market share by 50 percent
- → Productivity by 75 percent as measured by individual product outputs
- → Sales by 50 percent
- → Patient satisfaction by 75 percent
- → Employee retention by 50 percent
- → New hires successfully completing full orientation and initial training by 75 percent

→ We will decrease:
- → Fraud and waste by 75 percent
- → Discrimination complaints by 50 percent
- → Legal costs by 50 percent

The creative process can be very stimulating and very exciting, as people use the energy of the group to trigger vast numbers of new ideas for solving problems, increasing organizational success, and improving working conditions. However, successful problem solving requires a step-by-step process, and leaders who fail to follow the steps through to completion may waste their creativity and the creativity of their people. They may find themselves hearing,

- ■ "Well, this is all great, but nothing ever happens after we come up with all of these great ideas."
- ■ "I have real work to be done, on things that will actually happen."

■ "I always enjoy these conversations, but they take time away from what I need to be doing. It would be different if any of this stuff ever happened."

Instead, leaders want to hear from their teams:

■ By developing these creative ideas, my workload has just been cut in half. This is great!
■ I am so happy we have worked to solve these problems. Now I have the promise of more efficiency, success, and profitability in the near future.
■ It is great to work with such creative and responsible people. Our company will go far.
■ Now that we have transformed our working processes, we will be able to meet our targets.
■ I am now clear on what we are trying to accomplish. It is great to have aligned all of our efforts.
■ We have a far greater chance of success now that we have engaged all of our creativity together.
■ Not only have we come up with lots of great ideas, but we are clear on what steps we need to take to become successful.

Progressing through the steps in this chapter will help to ensure that these will be your organization's perfect phrases.

CHAPTER 4

Discovering the "Magic"

Creativity requires accessing the right brain through divergent thinking activities *before* using the left brain for the convergent activities—evaluating, prioritizing, decision making, and action planning—that are more familiar to us in the working world, those that were covered in the last chapter. This truth bears repeating. And so, by this point in the book, you have no doubt heard evidence of it a number of times, and perhaps you have used some of the perfect phrases from earlier chapters to challenge yourself and others toward greater divergence and thus greater creativity.

Furthermore, as Frans Johansson, author of *the Medici Effect*, indicates, "Quantity of ideas leads to quality of ideas." The best predictor of groundbreaking papers in science, agrees Dean Simonton, coauthor of *Creativity and Genius*, is who has published the most, has had breakthrough papers produced at random points throughout her or his career, and is cited more in other people's papers. So, not only are right-brain divergent strategies necessary, but strategies that generate lots and lots of ideas have the best chance of triggering the greatest creativity. So, in this chapter, I spell out a wide range of activities that can stimulate creative thinking, that energize groups to generate multitudes of ideas, and that bring the "magic" into teams' work together as they aim for transformational change.

There are a few things to remember, however. For one thing, keep creativity groups small. Frans Johansson points to research that indicates that the larger the group, the fewer the ideas. This is because people have to wait to speak their ideas, and as a result, they can't keep the idea-generating momentum going or hold the ideas in their short-term memory. Also, hold off on evaluating until you have generated a lot of ideas, so as to create an environment in which:

- All ideas can be heard, no matter how crazy they seem at the time.
- People are supported and their ideas are accepted, or at least heard.
- Everyone can have some fun and laugh a bit.
- Team members can draw on the deeper meanings, or their more spiritual or inspired selves.
- There is a spirit of honesty and willingness to fully hear others' ideas.
- Difference is a virtue.

Brainstorming

Brainstorming, first described by Alex Osborne in 1941, is well known to most people as an idea-generating strategy. But brainstorming can be structured in a variety of ways, depending on the setting, the needs, and the particular participants. In most cases, the ideas generated will be written on flipcharts, sticky notes, or index cards. What follows are perfect phrases for implementing Michael Michalko and others' ideas on different types of brainstorming. We begin with brainstorming warm-ups. We then move to basic brainstorming, which most people are familiar with, although many of the other brainstorming strategies are not as biased toward extraverted people.

Perfect Phrases for Brainstorming

Brainstorming Warm-Ups

To get team members into the spirit of brainstorming, generating laughs and fun, Michael Michalko suggests conducting some sort of warm-up activity that gets people out of their left-brain "work" state and into a playful, wacky, innovation-generating state. For instance, ask everyone to:

➜ Bring in baby pictures, then say, "Try to match the pictures with the participants who brought them."

➜ Draw a personal symbol that represents your view of creativity. Share and explain your symbol.

➜ Draw an animal, bird, insect, or fish as the corporate symbol for your business or organization. Defend your choice.

➜ Imagine that you have been fired and are now reapplying for your job. This activity focuses participants on what they might do to improve.

➜ In competing groups, use Popsicle sticks to create the largest structure you can. Whichever group builds the largest structure wins. The aim of this activity is to demonstrate that those who were most successful experienced the most failures.

Basic Brainstorming

After deciding on and posting or describing the problem, say:

→ Let's throw out as many ideas as quickly as possible on ways to solve the problem and let's build on one another's ideas.
→ Let's not evaluate or criticize any of the ideas.
→ Let's think outside the box.
→ I'd like to come up with as many new ideas as we can.
→ Let's offer any ideas that come to mind.
→ Let's generate as many new options as we can think of.
→ Let's have some fun coming up with ideas.
→ Don't be afraid to come up with off-the-wall ideas.
→ Anything goes! As many and as varied ideas as you can think of.
→ Let's aim for coming up with lots and lots of ideas. We can weed out those we don't want later.

Wacky to Workable Brainstorming

After posting or describing the problem, write the following titles at the top of three flipcharts: Wacky, Interesting, and Workable. Then say:

→ We are going to throw out as many wacky, wild, or impractical ideas as we can imagine as quickly as possible. The wackier, the better. There should be lots of laughter and fun in the process.
→ The sky is the limit.
→ Have some fun; laugh; get wackier.
→ Here are some wacky ideas to prime the pot, as examples (leader then states some).

Record people's ideas on the "Wacky" flipchart. After a substantial number of ideas have been generated, say:

→ Let's look at these wacky ideas and discuss how each of them might be turned into something interesting, something that makes you say, "Hmmm . . . maybe there's something to this."

Record these ideas on the "Interesting" flipchart. After generating many "interesting" ideas, ask:

→ How might we turn these interesting ideas into something workable, something that is worth trying?

Record these ideas on the "Workable" flipchart.

Brainstorming Bulletin Board

On a publicly situated bulletin board, write a problem or a question and make the following requests:

→ Please post your idea in response to this problem on the bulletin board in the lunchroom.
→ Please return to the bulletin board periodically to review others' suggestions.
→ Then, use other people's ideas to stimulate more of your own ideas.
→ And, please post these new ideas as well.

Brainstorming Consultant

→ Write a problem on an index card.
→ Pass it to the person next to you, who will have 60 seconds to write solution ideas, thus serving as your consultant.
→ Keep passing the card around until you get your problem card back with all of the "consultants'" ideas.

Solo Brainstorming

→ Use a package of index cards.
→ Write as many ideas as possible on the cards, one on each card, as quickly as you can.
→ Produce a great quantity of cards and ideas without evaluating any of them.
→ When you have come up with as many ideas as you can:
    → Sort them.
    → Evaluate them.
    → Combine them.
    → Free associate with them.
    → Reverse them.
    → Rearrange them.
    → Adapt them.
    → Transpose them.
    → Substitute them.
    → Consider them from another point of view.
    → Draw or diagram them.
    → Make a metaphor for them.
    → Force connections between two or more of the cards' ideas.
    → Imagine what a critic would say about them.
    → Modify them.
    → Sleep on the idea(s).

Brain Sketching

Say:

→ Sketch your ideas.
→ Collect pictures, photographs, or diagrams that are related to the problem.

→ Put everything up on an image board so that you can see them clearly.

→ Rearrange them in various ways until ideas come.

Brain Writing

Give everyone 3 × 5 cards, and say:

→ Write one idea on each card.

→ Pass that card to the person on your right.

→ That person will read your card as a stimulation card, will write down any new ideas that come to her or him on blank cards, and will then pass all the cards to the right.

→ We will keep passing the cards and brain writing for 20 to 30 minutes or until everyone has exhausted her or his ideas.

After 20 to 30 minutes, collect the cards. Have the group tape them to the wall, eliminate the duplicates, categorize the ideas, and prioritize them by putting sticky dots next to their favorite ideas.

Idea Pool

This is the same as brain writing, except that people put ideas on as many cards as possible and put the idea cards in the center of the table. When others run out of ideas and need stimulation, they pick a card from the pile to stimulate more of their own ideas.

Round Robin Silent Sharing

As a variation on brain writing or an idea pool, people put ideas on as many cards as possible and put their idea cards in a pile to their right. Only if the person to their right runs out of ideas does he or she pick up a card as a stimulus to more ideas. She or he then writes more ideas on new cards.

Gallery

Put flipchart sheets along a wall or around the room. Say:

➜ Write your ideas on the flipchart sheets.
➜ When you run out of ideas, rotate around to the next sheet, see what others have written, and write ideas in response.
➜ When you again run out of ideas, rotate around to the next sheet and do the same. And so on.
➜ You can write the ideas or draw or diagram the ideas.

Three Plus

Say:

➜ Write three ideas at the top of three sheets of paper.
➜ Pass the sheets to the person next to you, who will write ideas that improve on what you have written, and will then pass the sheets on.
➜ The next person will do the same, and so on.
➜ If you can't think of an improvement, write a new idea.
➜ Continue until the sheets return to their original owners.

Wall of Ideas or Write It, Say It, Stick It Up

Say:

➜ Write as many ideas as you can think of on sticky notes and pass them to me (or the group leader).
➜ I will put them on the wall (or on a flipchart).
➜ When everyone has exhausted her or his ideas, we will all gather at the wall.
➜ We will then organize the ideas in a meaningful way:
    ➜ Clustering them into themes and categories
    ➜ Labeling the categories

→ Using sticky dots to mark our favorites
→ Prioritizing our favorites

Brainstorming Notebooks

Give everyone a notebook. Say:

→ Please write at least one idea in your notebook each day.
→ At the end of each week, for four weeks, we will switch notebooks and continue putting one idea per day in them, also responding to what others have put in the notebooks.
→ After four weeks, I will collect the notebooks, categorize the ideas, and write a summary for the group to discuss.

Stravinsky Effect

In response to a challenge, say:

→ Please write eight ideas on the 3 × 5 cards I am passing out, one idea per card.
→ I will then collect and shuffle the cards and distribute three cards to each of you (but not your original cards).
→ I will put the leftover cards face up in the center of the table.
→ You will then prioritize your cards.
→ You may exchange any of your cards that have ideas that you don't like or that you like less than others with a card in the center of the table.
→ After you have done this, compare your cards with the other participants' cards, and exchange at least one of your cards for one of theirs that you like better.
→ Next, cluster with other people. Clusters may have as many people as you would like, but no cluster may keep any more than three cards.

➔ Finally, prepare a creative way to present your cluster's three ideas to the larger group (prepare a poster, bumper sticker, slogan, logo, T-shirt, TV commercial, song, or something else).

SIL (Silently write, Integrate, Learn)

In response to a problem, say:

➔ Silently write as many ideas as you can think of to solve the problem.
➔ Now, two people will each read one of their ideas out loud.
➔ The rest of the group will try to integrate their two ideas into one idea.

After working at this integration, say:

➔ Someone else needs to read an idea.
➔ Now, try to integrate that idea with the one you created in the previous step.

Keep this process going until all of the ideas have been read and integrated into one final solution. It may not be possible to integrate all of the ideas, but at least all of the ideas and all of the participants will get a fair hearing.

Open Meeting

Distribute the meeting agenda prior to the meeting. When people arrive for the meeting, say:

➔ There are flipchart sheets around the room.
➔ Please identify an issue that needs to be discussed that is related to the agenda. Say it out loud and write it on one of the flipchart sheets.

When the group has exhaustively identified the issues, say:

→ Now you may volunteer to work on an issue by signing up on its sheet.
→ Gather with others who are also interested in that issue. Work on it and post your ideas.
→ If you personally run out of ways to contribute solutions to that particular issue, you may let your feet do the talking and switch to another group to assist on its issue.

Storyboarding

Say:

→ I have posted a "topic card" (with a solution or problem) on the wall, along with a "purpose card" that outlines the purpose of working on this issue.
→ Please identify headings related to the topic, write the headings on cards, and post the heading cards underneath the topic and purpose cards.
→ Heading cards may include major issues, attributes, or solution categories (including a miscellaneous card).
→ Then, brainstorm ideas, solutions, and thoughts in response to the problem or solution statement.
→ Write the ideas on cards and put these on cards under the headers.
→ Let's brainstorm as many ideas as possible, hitchhiking on other ideas and combining them.
→ We will add more headers as necessary.

Take a photo of the completed board so as to preserve it for future work.

Borrowing and Combining

David Murray, in *Borrowing Brilliance,* points out that historically the most creative people worked together or met together regularly in order to share ideas, learn from one another, and build on what others had created. They intentionally created situations in which they could *borrow* other people's ideas in order to add to them and combine them in new ways. He urges us to do that as well: to beg, borrow, and steal ideas and combine them into something new. The further away from our subject we borrow, he says, the more creative the solution becomes. We can begin with our own domain and with our competition's. But we can then look further away, toward places that are tied together with ours by problems similar to ours.

Most extraordinary new ideas happen at the intersections between different professions, rather than at the center of individual professions. Johansson calls this the "Medici effect," from the Medici family in Italy, who funded creators from a wide range of disciplines. By drawing them together into one city to converse and work near one another, the family effectively began the Renaissance. No one in those days considered this sharing and using of others' ideas to be stealing or plagiarism. As Murray says, "If you steal from one author, it's plagiarism. If you steal from many, it's research." He urges us to keep our eyes open, to hone our observational skills, and to look for the making and breaking of patterns. As you review the perfect phrases given here, you will notice that generating many ideas through brainstorming may still play an important role during the borrowing and combining processes. Murray further suggests that we surround ourselves with creative thinkers from whom we can learn. Thomas Edison said that he started from where others left off. Lincoln indicated that he could learn something from everyone he met. Steve Jobs of Apple said, "Why join the Navy if you can be a pirate?"

Perfect Phrases for Borrowing and Combining

We might, therefore, ask or declare:

→ Whom can we borrow from?
→ Who are our competitors? What are they doing?
→ Who is there in my profession that I might confer with or observe?
→ Who are not our competition and not in my profession, but have problems to solve that look like ours? What solutions have they come up with?
→ I want to surround myself with creative thinkers. Whom might I include in that group?
→ Whom might I meet with regularly to bounce ideas off of?
→ I want to develop a creativity group outside of my workplace with very smart people from different professions.
→ I want to stay open to as many new ideas as possible.
→ How might I carefully observe everything around me so as to see what I might borrow to solve this problem?
→ I want to be a lifelong learner and voraciously devour information from all different fields in order to discover answers that might work in my situation.

Michael Michalko offers further ideas for taking known information and *dividing, combining, or manipulating* it to offer new entry points for solving problems. For instance, he suggests that when we find ourselves stuck, we might use *Mind Mapping* or *SCAMPER*.

Mind Mapping

Mind Mapping helps us to map our impressions and thoughts in order to provoke new ideas. We can:

- Use think bubbles on big paper or a blackboard to illustrate or create patterns and relationships.

- Group the bubbles.

- Use arrows to connect bubbles.

- Use key words that capture essences.

- Make connections and links.

- Cluster ideas.

- Then study the map, put it away for an incubation period, and later return to it.

SCAMPER

In order to transform any object, service, or process into something new, we can first identify the challenge, and then use each of the following SCAMPER steps:

Substitute something (for example, other places, rules, ingredients, materials, processes, procedures, powers, approaches, formats, or scenarios). We can say:
- ❑ Let's substitute something—another idea or substance or person.

- ❑ Let's change the rules.
- ❑ I want to try some other ingredients or materials.
- ❑ We could substitute other processes or procedures.
- ❑ Let's think about how it would work in another place.
- ❑ I want to consider a different approach.
- ❑ What else might work instead?
- ❑ Let's consider some other part that might be more helpful than this.

Combine it with something else (for example, other ideas, purposes, assortments, blends, units, articles, packages, materials, appeals, products, or resources). We can say:

- ❑ Let's combine some of these ideas.
- ❑ How about combining purposes?
- ❑ We might consider using an assortment.
- ❑ Let's think about using a blend, an alloy, or an ensemble.
- ❑ I am considering combining units. What would that look like?
- ❑ Let's merge another article with this.
- ❑ Have we considered how we could package some combination?
- ❑ Let's see what happens when we combine in order to multiply possible uses.
- ❑ Let's consider combining materials.
- ❑ How might we combine appeals?

Adapt something to it. We might say:

- ❑ What else is like this?
- ❑ Let's consider what other ideas this suggests.
- ❑ I am looking back to see if the past offers a parallel.
- ❑ I'd like to find something I could copy.

- ❑ What could I emulate?
- ❑ I am looking for an idea to incorporate.
- ❑ What other process(es) could be adapted?
- ❑ I want to think about other things that could be adapted.
- ❑ Let's think about other contexts in which our concept might work.
- ❑ Let's think about other fields outside of our own—how might we incorporate what they are doing?

Modify or **M**agnify it (for example, ideas, processes, contexts, behaviors, markets, adaptations from nature, or materials). We can say:

- ❑ Let's consider what can be magnified, made larger, or extended.
- ❑ I am going to try exaggerating or overstating some of these to see what happens.
- ❑ Let's think about what can be added. What happens if we give it more time?
- ❑ I want to make it stronger, higher, or longer.
- ❑ Let's add greater frequency or extra features and see what happens.
- ❑ What might add extra value?
- ❑ I want to consider what might be duplicated.
- ❑ How might we carry this idea to a dramatic extreme?
- ❑ Let's think about altering this for the better.
- ❑ What might we modify?
- ❑ I am trying to think of a new twist that I haven't yet considered.
- ❑ Let's try changing the meaning, color, motion, sound, odor, form, or shape.

- ❑ I want to try out some new names and see what we come up with.
- ❑ Are there any other changes we can think of?
- ❑ Let's consider what changes might be made in the plans, in the process, or in the marketing.
- ❑ What other form could this take that might be helpful? What other packaging could we use?
- ❑ Let's think about what happens if we combine the package with the form.

Put in some other use. We might say:
- ❑ I want to consider other possible uses for this.
- ❑ Let's also consider new ways to use it as is.
- ❑ Might we find other uses if we modified it?
- ❑ I am trying to think about what else could be made from this.
- ❑ Are there other extensions? Other markets?

Eliminate something. We could say:
- ❑ Let's consider what might happen if this were smaller.
- ❑ What could we omit?
- ❑ I am considering what happens if I divide it, split it up, or separate it into different parts.
- ❑ What if I understate it?
- ❑ Let's think about streamlining it, making it into a miniature, condensing it, compacting it, subtracting from it, or deleting something.
- ❑ I am going to see what happens if we eliminate some of the rules.
- ❑ What's not necessary?

Reverse or **R**earrange it. We can say:

→ What other arrangement might be better?
→ I am wondering how we might interchange components.
→ Let's consider another pattern or another layout.
→ What other sequence might work better?
→ I want to think about changing the order.
→ I am considering the benefits of transposing cause and effect.
→ Let's see what happens if we change the pace or change the schedule.
→ Can I transpose positive and negative?
→ What are the opposites?
→ What are the negatives?
→ Let's try turning it around—up instead of down or down instead of up.
→ I'm going to try it backwards.
→ How might I reverse roles?
→ What if we did the unexpected?

Intersections and Random Connections

Johansson offers thoughts on combining ideas at intersections or creating spaces where wildly different ideas can bump into and build upon one another, whether they be different "disciplines, cultures, [or] domains in which one can specialize through education, work, hobbies, traditions, or other life experiences." For instance, he says, "connecting two fields [or disciplines] sets off an exponential increase of unique concept combinations, a veritable explosion of ideas." The many possibilities of one field combine with the many possibilities of another in a multiplicative way.

Creativity comes from combining such concepts or fields in an unusual fashion, and it is often a random process, making it difficult to trace the origin of an insight. Sarnoff Mednick indicates that "the more mutually remote the elements of a new combination, the more creative the process or the solution." We want to look for a "ha ha" reaction, rather than an "aha" or "ah" reaction. *The* big idea may come in a moment and may seem to result from blind luck. However, careful observation indicates that ideas generally result from a "prepared mind," which is created when a person becomes an expert, thinks about a problem intensively for a long period of time, and then stops thinking about it to allow ideas to incubate. The question, then, is how to find the unusual or creative combinations. Many authors suggest ideas for how to find these combinations. Some of their ideas are presented in the perfect phrases offered here.

Perfect Phrases for Creating Intersections, Randomly Combining Concepts, or Forcing Connections

→ I am going to expose myself to a *range of cultures*, so that I:
  → Find other ways to view things.
  → Don't stay wedded to a particular point of view (for example, an ethnic, class, professional, or organizational culture).
  → Become fluent in various languages.
→ Let's *learn "differently"* to counteract what we've learned in school; for instance:
  → Avoid schools and experts who get us wedded to one particular view.
  → Learn as many things as possible without getting stuck in a particular way of thinking about those things.

→ Expose ourselves to many different bright people and talk with them about many things, including our challenge; listen carefully; and draw out their creativity.

→ Commit to teaching ourselves.

→ Broaden our education to many fields.

→ Spend significant amounts of time reading and drawing, learning and experimenting.

→ I want to hire people who *diversify* their *occupations*:

→ Moving between or switching fields, jobs, projects, or hobbies so as to notice the intersections.

→ "Wasting time" on hobbies or things that are unrelated to work.

→ I am going to become *intentional about becoming creative*, rather than relying on chance.

→ Let's *reverse our assumptions*:

→ First, we will intentionally direct our minds to take unusual paths while thinking about a situation.

→ Then, we will think about a situation, product, or concept related to that particular challenge.

→ Next we will write down assumptions associated with that situation.

→ The next step is really important: we want to reverse those assumptions.

→ Now we can think about how to make those reversals meaningful.

→ I plan to try on *multiple perspectives*:

→ View things from a variety of different angles.

→ Apply ideas to someone or something else (for example, a famous artist, cook, singer, or ballplayer).

→ Create constraints (for example, imagining not being able to speak or walk or use my hands).

→ Let's *introduce randomness* into our thinking by searching for or forcing connections in unlikely places and seeing where those connections lead. For instance, let's:

→ Look up three words in the dictionary at random, and attempt to tie them together.

→ Choose a word or phrase randomly from a dictionary or a random word list, preferably something tangible (for example, tail wagging dog), and brainstorm ways to answer our problem question (for example, how might we work more efficiently?) by applying the random word to the situation (for example, how might tail wagging dog help us to get rid of distractions?).

→ Take a *thought walk*—through the office, into the parking lot, down the street—looking for objects, situations, or events that we can compare to our subject metaphorically, making as many metaphors as we can between our list and the topic, and looking for ways to transfer principles into ideas to solve the problem.

→ Pick up random items (or note them or borrow or buy them) that are unrelated to the problem. Then write the characteristics of each item and force connections between these characteristics and the problem we are working on.

→ Buy a magazine that we typically don't read, select a page, and try to force connections between what is on the page and what we are working on.

→ Play with switching nouns and verbs.

→ Collect and store ideas—advertisements, quotes, designs, ideas, questions, cartoons, pictures, and so on.

→ Pick a magazine article at random.

→ Select a shape and focus on it for a day.

→ Collect and bring out famous quotations when we need a new idea, then ponder the quotations and write our thoughts.

→ Play "what if"—in response to a challenge, list as many "what if" scenarios as we can, and try to answer questions posed by the scenarios. Then use directed imagination—take one theme in our "what if" scenario, identify attributes, and force connections between our field and that theme.

→ Let's *force connections*:

  → Between ideas, subjects from unrelated fields, problems, elements of extreme ideas, and/or domains that we write on slips of paper and draw from a jar.

  → By combining unrelated objects, goods, or services; for instance, by choosing the first letter of our last names, identifying an object starting with that letter, and mingling with others in the group to combine our two objects into something new.

  → By using color questioning—for instance, using de Bono's hats or other colors to represent neutral, positive, creative, hopeful, and negative perspectives and brainstorming through all the colors when considering a problem or solution.

  → By picking a famous person and considering how that person would approach the problem.

  → Through "crossbreeding":

    • Taking four boxes of slips of paper with random names of plants, objects (some of which are business-related), animals, and job descriptors.

    • Taking one slip from each box and making hybrids of them.

    • Drawing pictures of the hybrids.

- Thinking about what each hybrid does, its unique strengths and weaknesses.
- Considering how these hybrids relate to the question or problem.

→ By sending people out to observe people in an unrelated field and asking them to come back with ideas for their own field.

→ By selecting a random word, defining its attributes, then forcing connections between these attributes and the problem to come up with ideas (choose random words from a dictionary, use a random word list, or open a book to any page and point to a word; the best words can be visualized, are simple, and are rich in connections).

→ By creating a fantasy board of directors of powerhouse business leaders; researching them; getting their photos to post; taking notes on their lives, their obstacles and how they overcame those obstacles; then "consulting" them when we have a problem (How would Henry Ford resolve this problem?); and expecting to find ideas in the thoughts and words of others.

→ By drawing a clock, listing 12 attributes that are related to our challenge, assigning the attributes to the clock's numbers; throwing dice to select two attributes and free-associating the connections between them; and finally searching for links between these attributes and our challenge.

→ By drawing the attributes in abstract graphics, in different colors, on different index cards; then put them on the table, and rearrange them randomly, looking for connections, ideas, or thoughts.

→ By finding analogies between two dissimilar areas of experience (two different professions, a profession and an object, animals, food items, tools [for example, "If your problem were a lawn, what would the weeds be?"]):

- Personal analogy, or identifying with some part of the problem and getting into it—wearing the problem's clothes, talking its language, eating its food, singing its songs, reciting its slogan and mottos. "How would I feel if I were . . . ?"
- Direct analogy, or comparisons and similarities between parallel facts and events in different fields or parallel worlds. State the challenge. Choose a key word. Choose a parallel or distant field. List images associated with the chosen field. Look for connections between the key word and these images. The parallel world must be something you know well.
- Symbolic analogy, or creating a visual image of the problem with no words or labels, perhaps by drawing it.
- Fantasy analogy, or fantasizing, in response to a problem, the best possible world with the most satisfying solution to the problem.

Attribute Analysis

Attribute analysis asks creative individuals or teams to consider the attributes of their issues, create categories under those attributes, and then combine those categories in all possible ways until new ideas pop up. For instance, if a team was looking for new concepts in health insurance/care, it would:

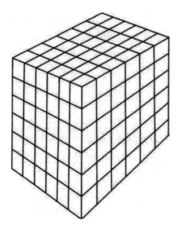

Figure 4.1

- Decide on attributes of health insurance (for example, cost, providers, or services covered).
- List all of the possible costs, all of the possible providers, and all of the possible services (or a range of each).
- Create a cube apparatus, with the various costs along one axis, various providers along another axis, and various services along the third axis.
- Examine the intersections of each of the blocks on the cube for ideas (see Figure 4.1).

Another way to conduct this exercise uses a chart format, like the one in Figure 4.2. After stating the subject of the problem under consideration:

- List the attributes in the top row.
- List as many alternatives as you can think of in the rows below.

■ Finally, combine from each of the alternative lists to see what is triggered (for example, patients in charge, at home, inexpensive, blissful).

Who's in Charge	Where	Cost	Pain Level
Doctors in charge	At health care facilities	Expensive	Painful
Nurses in charge	At home	Less expensive	Pain-free
Businesspeople in charge	At offices	Inexpensive	Less painful
Patients in charge	On the street	Free	Blissful
Health care advocates in charge	In department stores	Expensive	Painful
Social workers in charge	In restaurants	Less expensive	Pain-free
Psychologists in charge	At government offices	Inexpensive	Less painful
Accountants in charge	In a neighborhood	Free	Blissful

Figure 4.2

Individuals Whose Creativity Built Successful Companies

The following are people who succeeded as a result of being adept at intersections, combinations, and connections.

Richard Garfield

Richard Garfield, a math Ph.D. student, developed the game Magic, which led to an entire genre of games (Pokémon) that has become an international phenomenon. He:

- Combined the "games" world with the "collectibles" world.
- Developed many decks of cards.
- Produced different cards each year.

As a result:

- Players often buy a whole deck of cards just to get one card.
- Each time the game is played, players choose a selection of cards from their private collection to play with.
- Trading cards and the ability to play online has built an ever-expanding international community of players.

Orit Gadiesh

Orit Gadiesh leads Bain & Company, one of the world's leading strategy consulting firms, which aims to help organizations develop innovative growth strategies. Her success and that of those she consults with comes from:

- Not being intimidated by important people.
- Taking risks.
- Going against the crowd.
- Spending time on a variety of projects in different fields to create intersectional ideas.
- "Wasting time" on hobbies or things that are unrelated to work—which are then sometimes subconsciously integrated back into her work.
- Reading many books outside her field.

- Making people switch areas and fields, so as to get better at their area of expertise as a result of taking a chance and doing something else.
- Working on several different projects at once.
- Interacting with diverse groups of people.

Steve Miller

Steve Miller, former CEO and Chairman of Royal Dutch/Shell, the world's fourth-largest company, claims that if we want to generate creative ideas, we should:

- Hire people who make us uncomfortable or whom we dislike.
- Hire motivated and engaged people, even if we don't need them yet—we will find connections between their skills and the organization's needs.
- Depersonalize conflicts so as to take advantage of different disciplines, cultures, thinking styles, values, and attitudes.

Håkan Lans

Håkan Lans is a Swedish inventor who is responsible for designing a short-range coastal tracking system that is mandatory aboard large international voyaging ships and all passenger ships and is used in a surveillance technique for air traffic control. He:

- Learned differently—he was self-taught in virtually every discipline of technology and engineering.
- Was adept at finding intersections between many of those fields, combining ideas from different fields.
- Was a prolific producer of ideas and innovations.

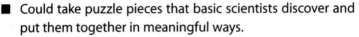

- Could take puzzle pieces that basic scientists discover and put them together in meaningful ways.
- Relentlessly pursued the best of the ideas.

Marcus Samuelsson

Marcus Samuelsson, beginning when he was a 24-year-old cook for a well-respected New York City Swedish restaurant, took that restaurant from one star to three stars after the experienced head cook died. He:

- Has charisma, energy, and persistence.
- Was adopted from Ethiopia by a Swedish family, looked different, and never saw his Swedish town as the be-all and end-all.
- Traveled extensively while he was young, eating many different foods.
- Received culinary education in several countries.
- Learned to speak many different languages fluently.
- Traveled around the world on a cruise ship, eating and cooking different good food at every port, then applying his unique perspectives and experiences to those culinary experiences.
- Diversified the kitchen staff, sacrificing experience for open attitudes.
- Combines foods from all over the world.
- Looks for related concepts in distant places and unexpected areas of cooking, and tries to reconcile these far-flung ideas into recipes.

CHAPTER 5

Creative Spaces

How many times have you been summoned for training to a dreary basement hotel meeting room or to a dreary room in your office building? Or to a room with seats all in rows facing the speaker at the front? Or even to a state-of-the-art training room that has all the high-tech equipment one could dream of, but that has walls, seats, and carpeting in an unrelenting shade of beige or gray?

And how much of that training has been related to creativity? Is it really possible to be creative in a beige room with beige carpeting and no natural light? Can we draw on our whole selves—our most creative selves, our divergent selves—in an environment that is devoid of creativity, divergence, and creative energy? In a space that doesn't feed our souls? That has no heart? That doesn't encourage interpersonal interaction? I don't know about you, but most of my experience of training has been in rooms such as this.

On the other hand, when training has been scheduled in environments with a heart and soul, the difference in the spirit present in the room—both my spirit and the participants' spirits—has been striking! I was lucky enough during recent trainings to be looking out a very large window at a panoramic view of the green trees and snow-capped mountains of Colorado and later at Mission Bay in San Diego. Those trainings were the epitome of triggering the creative spirit! Talk about inspiring! And all of us left the trainings revitalized rather than depleted.

I think we have to ask ourselves questions related to the spaces in which we try to create, and we have to consider how those spaces affect our ability to be creative. For instance:

- Can we really believe that *many answers exist*, or can we pursue *divergent* thinking, if we are in an environment that is devoid of stimulation, with no expression of what's optimal for a working environment? Don't we need a variety of stimulations in order to trigger and to help us find a variety of ideas?

- Can we really find our "call" or get into the "flow" in a space that is devoid of "spirit" and of any of the "higher" things in life?

- Are we really *valuing ourselves* or the creativity that we are engaged in if we deprive ourselves of light, art, color, and fresh air?

- Is there any chance that we can bring our *whole selves* into the creative process, including our inner child, if there is nothing in the meeting space that can support our emotional, physical, spiritual, visually artistic, auditory, or nature intelligences?

- Can we really stay *open* to differences, whether those are different points of view, different experiences, or different sources of information, in a monochromatic, monofunctional room?

- Is there any possibility of maximizing the *power of the group or community* when everyone is isolated in his or her individual, gray metal cubicle, and creative gatherings would interrupt everyone else's work?

Clearly, there are companies, organizations, and training experts who answer each of these questions with a resounding, "No!" and intentionally seek out or create environments that support creativity. For instance, I am sure many of us have heard about training sessions or creativity meetings that were held:

■ In mountain retreat centers
■ Overlooking the beach
■ In fancy retreat centers in the Bahamas or in Puerto Rico, with boats and pools and scuba equipment available
■ In "playrooms" supplied with all kinds of children's toys and/ or children's art supplies
■ In rooms with comfortable chairs that don't overtax the bodies that will be spending a good deal of time in them
■ In intentionally designed hallways or corridors with groupings of chairs and tables or niches for groups to meet

Sometimes these training sessions or creativity spaces and meetings include activities that challenge participants to test their limits in all areas of their lives, communicating the idea that our heads are simply not enough if we are to be creative. These activities require environments beyond the hotel ballroom or organization's conference room. For instance:

■ Ropes experiences that challenge people's fears and physical capacities
■ Reflection retreats in the out-of-doors that challenge participants' abilities to be alone with themselves, to listen internally, to be still, and to hear answers
■ Rock and mountain climbing experiences or long hikes and bike rides that build teamwork and challenge people's confidence in their physical abilities

■ Games that introduce lightheartedness, playfulness, and laughter, and that encourage people to get to know one another as more than just who they are at work.

Hans Larsson, president of Enator, for instance, designed his company's building to "cultivate the bent of mind that is ready to grapple with problems." The building fosters spontaneous interactions and innovation. People feel free to be themselves. They meet perceptual problems at every turn. Wherever they look, they see the unexpected:

■ There are no rectangular rooms.
■ A cloud-filled sky is drawn on the floor.
■ Trompe l'oeil paintings on the walls suggest three-dimensional spaces.
■ Portholes and panes of glass in various walls or other places offer views of other rooms or floors.
■ Zigzagging corridors and geometric shapes are everywhere.
■ Rooms break convention—for instance, in one room, tables are made from a grand piano.
■ There are none of the usual visual guides (such as signs)—if you want to figure out where to go, you have to ask someone, which stimulates conversation and connections.

Imagine the creativity that could be stimulated in an environment such as Enator's!

Perfect Phrases for Developing Creativity-Enhancing Environments

Leaders who want to encourage creativity in their organizations, teams, or retreats need to develop or seek out creativity-enhancing environments. They might say to themselves and their teams:

→ Let's find a space that makes us laugh.

→ I think better when I am comfortable.

→ I need to see color and light if I am to create something new!

→ Where could we hold our creativity meeting that everyone would love being?

→ Let's meet in a place that has both quiet, calm spaces for reflection and crazy lights, colors, and noises to stimulate our wild side.

→ I love being out in nature—I do my best thinking there.

→ What if we found a meeting place that had walking trails, beautiful vistas, and calm, green glades?

→ Perhaps we need to rethink our own workspace—we need to add some artwork and "nature" places where we can sit and reflect.

→ I'd like to add comfortable seating areas in the hallways where we could meet spontaneously when we have an idea or want to ask others for ideas.

→ I want a workspace that feeds all of me—body, spirit, soul, emotions, thinking, child, vision, and smell.

→ Let's create that kind of space, or find a space for our creativity meetings that has most of those elements.

→ I'd like to build a playroom, with things that children like to do and play with (colors, balls, paints, games, food) to trigger people's playful side when creating.

➡ Let's cover the lunch tables with paper and leave out markers and paints. Everyone can draw, write, and add on to others' ideas.

➡ I know of a company that had a labyrinth that people could walk in order to regain their serenity and focus their thoughts and find answers. Maybe we could develop one.

➡ What about building a Japanese garden or a sculpture garden? Those soothe the spirit.

➡ Or couldn't we create a walking trail that was beautifully landscaped? Then people could get some exercise and be in a beautiful place to reflect.

➡ I'd like everyone to name her or his favorite place, and then list all of the characteristics of that place that make her or him happy. And let's commit to adding some of those things to our environment as a way of valuing ourselves.

➡ We need to build in time and space to reflect and to sit quietly, rather than valuing only rushing around at breakneck speed.

➡ We have all been to great retreat centers—what part of those environments might we recreate here?

➡ I commit to recreating my workspace into one that feeds my soul, heart, and spirit, rather than only my mind.

➡ We need some space for downtime in our building.

➡ Let's make the lunchroom more like a nice restaurant and forbid any "work talk" there.

➡ We need to get out of the office more often, to shift our perspectives and points of view.

➡ I am going to add more color, more art, and more visually stimulating vistas to our workplace environment.

➡ We need to add some music in the hallways and dining area, something soothing but beautiful.

→ Perhaps there are some employees who would be more creative if they could listen to any music they wanted to—let's experiment with giving some of them access to their iPods and headphones as they work on projects.

→ We need to continually remind people of our vision—and that is not merely a "head" thing. Let's make some videos that really touch people's hearts and remind them of why we do what we do. We can have the videos playing at various places in the building.

→ How might we make our workspace more creative and enlivening?

Enhancing Virtual Environments

Research tells us that virtual environments can be as effective as in-person environments for learning, meeting, and training as long as we invest just as much time, money, inspiration, and potential for interaction in the virtual environments, and as long as we don't include more people in the virtual conversations than we would if the meetings were in person. Of course, because the people participating in virtual meetings are not always visible, we have to trust a great deal more that they will fully participate in the processes that we design.

Perfect Phrases for Enhancing Virtual Environments

People who design virtual environments for learning or creativity meetings could benefit from considering how they might:

→ Include visual and auditory stimulation and variety in the online environment.

→ Ensure that the virtual environment is just as beautiful, peaceful, and/or stimulating as any in-person environment they would create.

→ Include a great deal of stimulation to trigger varieties of ideas and divergent thinking.

→ Consider the spirit of the presentation and the conversation, perhaps including some time for reflection and for presenting the values behind what they really want to accomplish.

→ Encourage civil, respectful conversations that value each person.

→ Keep time limits respectful of the rest of people's work life and of the limits of people's ability to concentrate.

→ Ensure that the activities inspire people to bring all of themselves to the conversation: spirit, mind, body, feelings, visuals, sounds, and nature.

→ Include opportunities for the expression of enough divergence—of values, interests, points of view, lifestyles, ages, genders, and cultures—so that participants are exposed to many possibilities as they create.

→ Ensure that everyone has a voice, that there is a good deal of interaction, so that the group process can work its magic.

→ Use chat rooms for online brainstorming.

CHAPTER 6

Extreme Challenges

Extreme challenges stimulate creativity because they engage more of who we are than what we usually bring to work. These opportunities for creativity tap into our emotions, dreams, and unconscious, or, in outrageous or unconventional ways, challenge our teams to overcome workplace hurdles. Some of these challenges were mentioned in the last chapter (for example, ropes programs and rock climbing). These challenges help us to:

- Access unconscious and right-brain paths toward creativity
- Overcome blocks to building functional and creative teams
- Use all of ourselves in the creative effort

Tapping the Unconscious

James Adams, in *The Care and Feeding of Ideas*, reminds us that conscious thinking and problem solving help us to:

- Decide what to do and do it
- See life in the abstract and build realistic constructs without actual experience

■ Communicate with one another, using abstract language

However, conscious thinking and problem solving:

■ Can use only information that we've taken in with our senses and retained in our memory through experiences that we've had in life
■ Is restricted in speed to a rate approximating that of life
■ Is linear and occupied by one topic until it switches to another
■ Prefers complete information
■ Is influenced by emotional and behavioral factors
■ Does not always do what we might like it to do

In fact, Adams says, if we limit ourselves to conscious thinking and problem solving, we become so habitual and specialized in our problem solving that it becomes difficult for us to create new solutions in response to change. We need to exert a conscious effort to pursue new directions when we are faced with new situations, because in those situations, the brain is not as efficient as it is in business-as-usual situations. Furthermore, when we are facing new situations, we need to constantly remember that the information in our minds is not complete, and that it is also not the same as the information in the minds of the people around us. Herein lies the reason that we need to intentionally structure time to tap into our unconscious: because there we can accomplish higher-order processing without conscious awareness. As James Adams, Michael Michalko, and Victoria Colligan, Beth Schoenfeldt, and Amy Swift suggest in the strategies described in this chapter, we can tap into our unconscious through the intentional use of:

■ Meditating
■ Tuning in to our intuition
■ Setting up paradoxes

- Accessing our dreams
- Using visualization and imagination
- Accessing humor

Perfect Phrases for Tapping the Unconscious

Team leaders might use these strategies with their teams with the instructions that follow.

Meditation

→ Find a quiet place where you can relax and empty your mind.

→ Sit or lie down in a comfortable position.

→ Pay close attention to your body, slowly visualizing yourself breathing in and out, and relaxing more deeply each time you breathe out.

→ Now tune in to each part of your body, first visualizing all the muscles in your feet and telling them to relax, let go, and become loose and limp. Think about warmth and heaviness in your feet. [Repeat this instruction for each part of your body.]

→ Now you might [choose one or more of the following]:

  → Recall a time when you were at peace with yourself.

  → Visualize an inner sanctuary that you can recreate when you need to—your own special place, a happiness room.

  → Place your worries in the basket of a hot-air balloon and watch them float away from you.

→ Imagine a mental block you may be experiencing as something you are wearing (for example, a ring). Then take it off.
→ Repeat the OOOOOMMMMMM sound.
→ Visualize yourself doing a favorite hobby or sport that gives you great enjoyment.

Intuition

→ I want to encourage you to pay attention to your feelings and believe in their accuracy.
→ Can I suggest that you use your intuition to [choose one of the following, depending on the situation]:
  → Sense when a problem exists
  → Rapidly perform well-learned behaviors
  → Synthesize bits of data and experience into an integrated picture
  → Check the results of your rational analysis by tuning in to your "gut" feelings
  → Bypass in-depth analysis and come up with a quick solution
→ Let's talk about how you might develop your intuition and use it in combination with your reason.

Paradox

When faced with a problem, team leaders might ask team members to:

→ Convert the problem to a paradox by imagining its opposite or its contradiction.
→ Imagine both the problem and its paradox being true at the same time.

→ Discover the essence of the problem by thinking in book titles that express those paradoxes (focused desire; balanced confusion; connected pauses; unorganized gatherings; lead by following; win by losing; take risks but be conservative).

→ Find analogies to your problem or paradox in nature, the animal world, other professions, or somewhere else.

→ Decide on a unique feature of the analogy.

→ Consider the equivalent of that unique feature in your problem situation. From this may come a new idea.

Dreams

In response to a problem, in order to discover answers that teams do not know that they know, team leaders might say to the team:

→ For several evenings, formulate a question about your challenge and repeat it to yourself before drifting off to sleep.

→ When you wake up, reflect on your dreams. Wake up 30 minutes earlier if you don't remember your dreams.

→ Record your dreams in detail in a dream journal, and use color drawings when appropriate.

→ Ask yourself the following questions:

→ How were the people, places, and events in the dream related to my question?

→ Who were the key players in the dream?

→ How does this relate to my question?

→ Does the dream change the nature of the question?

→ What elements in this dream can help me solve my problem?

→ What associations does the dream conjure up that might help with my problem?

→ What is the answer from the dream?

→ Free-associate from one or two dream images or ideas, writing down whatever comes to mind.

→ Keep the diary current.

Visualization and Imagination

To trigger a team's creativity through visualization and imagination, a team leader might say one of the following:

→ Imagine that we are on top of a mountain (or in some other extreme location)—what ideas come now?

→ Let's make believe we are dogs (or some other extreme image). What might a dog say about our problem?

→ Close your eyes and visualize yourself in five (or ten) years. What images come to mind?

→ Visualize the company in five years. What picture do you get?

→ Imagine where you would like to be and what you would like to be doing in five (or ten) years.

→ Visualize where you would like the company to be and what you would like it to have accomplished in five (or ten) years.

→ Write your story (or that of your company)—what will happen in the next five (or ten) years?

→ Find people to join you on the journey. Tell five people—from an array of backgrounds, life experiences, ages, and regions—your vision. Have each of them write the story of your success.

→ Accept feedback. Say it out loud.

Magic Wand

We often wish that we had magic at our disposal to help us in coming up with creative solutions. Giving the following directions to your team members gives them the chance to pretend they do:

→ You have been given a magic wand.
→ The wand grants you any wish you desire.
→ Write three to five wishes on cards or sticky notes in response to the problem or topic.

Humor

Some people seem especially good at seeing the humor in situations. And, in fact, when trying to solve problems creatively, humor:

→ Reduces tension and allows us to take more risk
→ Helps us to respond to the positive and negative emotions involved in creativity and change (excitement, humor, fun, embarrassment, fear, and anxiety)
→ Helps with insecurity and uncertainty
→ Creates a playful, humorous environment

Team leaders might ask:

→ What could you do that is illegal, immoral, or something that you'll get fired for?
→ What would surprise or shock people about you?

Alternatively, leaders might tell jokes or funny stories related to the problem.

Using the Creative Arts

The creative arts also offer opportunities for involving the whole person in the creative endeavor. It should be no surprise to you that such art forms as:

- Video
- Drama
- Music
- Painting
- Drawing
- Creating collages
- Working with clay
- Story or fable telling
- Writing
- Dance and movement

among others, can help us to:

- Get beyond conscious thought
- Access our unconscious
- Connect with our important memories
- Become aware of our emotions
- Fully use our right brain
- Access visual knowledge and pictorial conceptions of reality
- Be touched emotionally, and therefore be further motivated
- Be moved to act on our higher aspirations
- Have fun
- Come up with a wider range and greater quantity of possible options

We might:

- Interact or have a dialogue with the images
- Talk about them

- Reflect on themes or moods that they trigger
- Think symbolically

Perfect Phrases for Using the Creative Arts

Leaders might say:

→ Let's draw an image of a solution (or a problem).

→ Here are some art supplies—as you imagine a solution, create it with these.

→ I think I will bring clay dough (or other art supplies) to our next meeting.

→ There are scissors, colored paper, and glue sticks (or any of a wide range of art supplies, foods, small outdoor objects, and other such items) in front of you.

- → I want you to use those items to create your image of the problem we are facing right now.
- → No words!
- → Use the same materials to create your image of possible solutions.
- → Again, no words! (Perhaps play music in the background as people work.)
- → You have 15 minutes. Then we will look silently at your creations, and write a few words or questions in response.
- → Finally, you will verbally present the meanings you were trying to communicate.

→ There are hundreds of interesting and/or bright objects (collect them from all categories—animals, shells, dolls, wood, and so on) in this *sand tray*.

- → Talk about the issue.
- → As you talk, play in the sand.
- → Create scenes in response to the issue.
- → Don't think too much!
- → Just play and have fun while you talk.
- → See what comes to you.

→ I have put magazines, scissors, glue, and poster board in front of you.
  - → As you think and talk about the problem, create a *collage*.
  - → Assign a word to your problem, and use it as the title for the collage.
  - → Present the collage to the group by saying, "Our problem is like _____ from the collage because . . . ."

→ I have put many art supplies in front of you. I want you to:
  - → Review the challenge, write it down, and reflect on it.
  - → Relax.
  - → Allow your intuition to offer images, scenes, and symbols about the situation.
  - → Draw a boundary around the challenge.
  - → Draw as your mind wants to draw—without conscious direction, perhaps using your opposite hand; be random and scribble.
  - → Draw as many images as you wish.
  - → Examine the drawing.
  - → Write down the first word that comes to mind for each image, symbol, scribble, line, or structure.
  - → Combine the words and write a paragraph; free-associate.
  - → Consider how what you wrote relates to your challenge.

➜ Now instead of drawing it out, just quiet your mind and allow images to come to you involuntarily. Then look for the link between your challenge and the images. Ask yourself:

  → What puzzles me?
  → Is there any relationship between the images and the challenge?
  → Are there any new insights?
  → What's out of place?
  → What disturbs me?
  → What do the images remind me of?
  → What are the similarities?
  → What analogies can I make?
  → What associations can I make?
  → What do the images resemble?

➜ Or instead of drawing it out, take a guided imagery tour. Make the images as clear and vivid as you can of:

  → Stories you can read that have answers for you.
  → Stories with places to find answers (inside a briefcase, a movie on a wall, a message in a bottle, a letter that the main character receives, three doors that you open one at a time to find answers; a wise advisor or mentor who loves you and that you talk with).
  → Write down your imagery.
  → Interpret the images and read the messages.
  → Apply the images and messages to your own situation.

➜ In order to prepare for any possible problems or solutions that may emerge, to prepare both for the bad and for the good, write a story in which you:

  → Build four or five future scenarios that take into consideration the main influences.
  → Develop the scenarios into stories or narratives by varying the forces that affect the decision.
  → Search for business opportunities within each scenario.

As Michael Michalko says, "The more possible futures you foresee, the more options you can create; the more options you have, the greater your chances of finding the unexpected opportunity."

Team Challenges

Team challenges require team members to work together, competing against other teams, in creating ideas and solutions to particular kinds of problems—and teams get to have fun and become fully engaged while doing so. Teams might use any of the perfect phrases or creativity activities presented so far in this book in facing or solving these challenges—all these activities require team members to work together, have fun while doing so, and be creative in coming up with solutions. Teams then present their solutions, are judged by a panel of experts, and receive a score and sometimes prizes. Perhaps most important, they evaluate themselves as a team—what they did well that assisted them in attaining their goals, and what they could improve on in future real-life challenges. For instance, they might be given the task of demonstrating consensus, good decision making, risk taking, or any number of other group process goals, and evaluating how well they did in demonstrating these team skills. During the challenges, facilitators act as team coaches and observe team dynamics and the team's success in achieving the focal goals of the training. The challenges may be used up front as an assessment of team functioning and knowledge, or as an active learning experience after information has been presented. The team challenges given here were suggested by Dolly Hinshaw, trainer and sales and marketing expert. Dr. Eriksen has added perfect phrases for carrying out the challenges.

Business Simulations

Business simulations aim to recreate real workplaces to test new skills or to enhance current skills in a safe setting. Depending on the audience and the focus of the training, business simulations allow participants to develop competencies that drive better organizational results. The teams are assigned a specific business project. To add a dimension of fun and to get participants out of their comfort zones, teams might be assigned a project in the entertainment or international travel industry. Project ideas might include:

- Designing a customer service program for a hospital
- Decreasing machinery downtime in a manufacturing process
- Developing a marketing campaign for a new product
- Improving employee morale
- Enhancing departmental communication
- Analyzing why the competition has a greater market share of available customers

Individuals may be motivated to participate in a business simulation because it will help them to:

- Contribute to major decisions
- Demonstrate qualities that are not part of their current function
- Practice problem-solving techniques
- Improve their leadership skills
- Appreciate the talents of their coworkers
- Learn competencies in order to accept new responsibilities
- Extend themselves beyond their comfort zone
- Enjoy a fun break away from routine activities
- Test their competitive spirit

- Upgrade their performance with new skills
- Build more self-confidence as presenters
- Assess their personal skills as a decision maker, risk taker, or team player

Perfect Phrases for Business Simulations

Leaders or facilitators of a sales team simulation, for instance, might say:

→ As you know, we have been trying to increase our sales by 30 percent.
→ We have divided you into teams, and we want you to become a sales team whose task is to generate as many ideas as possible about how to increase sales.
→ After 15 minutes of meeting, we will ask you to take a time-out and evaluate how you are doing as a sales team—what you are doing well, not doing well, and might improve.
→ You will then continue your simulation, using what you have discussed during the time-out to improve your group functioning.
→ We will stop your teams periodically for these self-evaluative time-outs.
→ Write your "improving sales ideas" on a flipchart.
→ Write what you have learned about improving how you operate as a sales team on another flipchart.
→ You will share both your sales ideas and what you have learned about being a sales team with the larger group.

If it is used as a pretest tool, this type of simulation could begin a longer training or problem-solving experience, and the reports at the end could focus on what participants would like to learn during the training or in general as employees. If it is used after sales instruction, this type of simulation gives participants the opportunity to actively practice what they have been taught in order to bring the learning alive and to discover problem areas that might warrant more instruction or guidance. As noted earlier, simulations can focus on any functional area of a business.

Program or Training Development

Program or training development challenges offer unique opportunities for customizing employee learning based on the company's real needs for improving efficiency, productivity, motivation, and performance. Leaders ask employees to choose one priority area and design training, education, and development opportunities that will remove barriers in the organization and enhance future organizational success. The experience helps to pinpoint employee frustrations, system inefficiencies, management oversight problems, insufficiencies in talent, and much more. Executive-level decision makers join the groups at certain points to hear the teams' proposals.

Ideas from past challenges have included training sessions or programs on how to:

- Initiate job-sharing programs to expedite project completion dates.
- Design incentive programs for motivating sales teams.
- Focus on the "customer experience."
- Improve break-room environments to improve morale.
- Ensure that performance evaluations are given in a timely way so that employees feel that their contributions are valued.

- Read a financial statement so as to make informed budgetary decisions (for middle managers).
- Advance technologically in order to keep up with the competition.
- Enhance marketing campaigns to educate consumers about new products and services.
- Create a new employee orientation program for better "first impressions."

Program-training challenges result in participants becoming:

- Motivated to offer contributions
- Empowered to make a difference
- Inspired to create innovative ideas for improving their workplace
- Proud to play a role in the positive and profitable future of the organization
- Committed to making changes

Such a challenge:

- Enhances leadership and communication skills
- Fosters improved teamwork and respect for individual talents
- Improves balance in managing work and personal time
- Improves productivity because of better systems and procedures
- Generates improved quality as a result of performance improvements
- Builds better customer relationships

Perfect Phrases for Program or Training Development

A group leader might say: We want to know what you think are the greatest internal challenges facing our company at this time—that is:

➜ Where are we as individuals, teams, or larger divisions falling down on the job?
➜ What is broken in our way of operating that needs fixing?
➜ What skills or competencies do we need to enhance in order to optimize our functioning?
➜ What roadblocks are hindering optimal performance?

We need to come up with solutions to these problems, and train our people in how to carry out those solutions. Your task is to:

➜ Become very clear on the problem(s).
➜ Identify and choose potential solutions to the problem(s).
➜ Develop a course or training experience for employees so that they will develop expertise in the problem(s) and solutions.
➜ Design an evaluation of the degree to which the employees have learned what they need to learn.
➜ Create an evaluation of the impact of their learning on solving the problem(s).
➜ The course must be interesting and engaging.
➜ The course must be designed with adult learning principles in mind.
➜ You may use consultants as you design the course and the evaluations.

In addition to these tasks, your overall goal is to function well together as a team.

→ We will circulate to offer support for teamwork, will stop the task periodically to check in with you on how you are doing as a team, and will ask you to evaluate your team functioning at the end of the tasks.

→ You will share with the larger group both your course and what you have learned about operating as a team.

If it is used as a pretest tool, this type of simulation could begin a longer training or problem-solving experience, and the reports at the end could identify what participants would like to learn during the training or in general as employees. If it is used after instruction on talent management, development, or teamwork, this type of simulation gives participants the opportunity to actively practice what they have been taught in order to bring the learning alive and to discover problem areas that might warrant more instruction or guidance. The courses designed could focus on any problem that is currently hindering a business or organization from operating optimally in a particular market.

Global Diversity Challenges

Global diversity challenges[1] build personal and professional relationships in a nonthreatening environment. Genuine personalities, diverse talent, different perspectives and experiences, varied cultures, and unique ideas come together in a creative process, resulting in collaborative goal setting and innovation. Global

---

1 There are many definitions or meanings of global diversity. The intended definition for this challenge is defined as, "Expansion of products and services from a single corporate location based anywhere in the world to other international markets."

diversity challenges bring together people of different cultures and backgrounds for business purposes such as:

- Integrating new acquisitions into the parent organization
- Learning how customers choose products or services in different international markets
- Discovering new resources for development and process strategies
- Reducing communication misunderstandings and misinterpretations that might occur because of language barriers
- Resolving problems within new business approaches
- Understanding the different infrastructures of companies in different countries
- Adapting products and services to local markets
- Identifying new products or services for expansion
- Developing unity and camaraderie within the workforce
- Appreciating cultural perspectives and nuances
- Building mutual respect for talent proficiencies

In global diversity challenges, teams:

- Comprise employees at all levels of the organization.
- Include representatives with a range of cultural experiences.
- Are assigned a focal topic.
- Consider different cultural perspectives in developing solutions for particular problems.
- Present their focal topic and insights on the collaborative process to the larger group.

After a recess, the facilitators make observations about the teams' experiences and ask the group for ideas on focal topics for the future. Participants might exchange cultural gifts that represent the progress they have made toward fulfilling the organizational vision and mission. Meals and snacks might incorporate cultural flavors to enhance the group's multicultural experience.

The diversity goals of the global diversity challenge might include:

- Cultivating meaningful values across cultural boundaries
- Developing understandable policies to reduce conflict
- Utilizing helpful technologies for communication
- Respecting culturally appropriate team behavior and body language
- Unifying individual, corporate, and national cultures
- Demonstrating the value of expanding business internationally
- Ensuring access to diverse talent with varying cultural viewpoints

Perfect Phrases for Global Diversity Challenges

When carrying out a global diversity challenge as part of the planning for expanding into different markets, leaders might say:

→ As you all know, we wish to expand into some different markets.

→ Any time organizations explore different markets, they have to consider the differences of those markets from their current markets.

→ In our case, the countries into which we wish to expand differ considerably from our home country.

→ There is no substitute for real-life experiences with people from various cultures.

→ However, in preparation for real-life experiences, we have invited people to this meeting who have knowledge both of our company and of the cultures and values of the markets into which we wish to expand.

→ Teams are composed of individuals with a range of cultures and values.

→ Let's begin by introducing ourselves.

  → State your name, age, gender, race, religion, ethnicity, and socioeconomic class. (You may opt out of identifying yourself within any of these categories if you feel that identifying yourself will put you at risk or if you feel reluctant to share the information.)

  → Next, indicate which of these are most salient in your work currently.

  → Finally, state ways in which your differences in any of these areas have hampered or enhanced your work.

Each team will then decide on a product to launch in an assigned cultural market, and will develop a plan for product development, production, marketing, and sales. Individuals on teams will periodically:

→ Evaluate how they are doing as a team in considering the cultural differences of their members.

→ Offer one another input on what would help in ensuring that all perspectives are heard.

→ Use conflict resolution strategies to ensure that conflicts among different cultural perspectives are resolved in a way that honors the value of the differing perspectives.

Each team will report its experiences as a team as well as its proposed strategies for expanding into the proposed market.

TV Challenges

TV challenges ask participants to play the roles of people in various television shows, such as *The Apprentice*, *CSI*, or *The Amazing Race*, as a means of solving a problem or building teamwork. As participants try to "win," they also aim to:

- Demonstrate role clarity
- Build trust and solve problems
- Illustrate their resourcefulness, time management, and endurance

Group leaders would:

- First, create a picture of the "game"
- Indicate the goals
- Establish the rules
- Coach teams through the process
- Finally, give prizes for both the solution and the process

Perfect Phrases for TV Challenges

For instance, leaders might say:

→ You have all seen *CSI*, in which a crime is committed and a team has to go out and investigate it. The team members gather information at the crime scene. They gather any other information that might be available from other sources. They interview people. They consider various possible scenarios and prioritize them or rule them out based on the available information. And they finally come to a conclusion about who is responsible and, in a very exciting show, chase the person down and bring her or him to justice.

→ You will emulate *CSI*. The problem (or crime) is
_____ . (It should be a problem that the company is experiencing currently if the goal is to work both on something practical and on team building, or it can be something like the following if people are from different companies and the goal is to build teamwork and critical-thinking skills.)

  → Suppose $125,000 has been stolen in an armed robbery at the local bank. Shots were fired, and the suspects fled the scene. The cops have found the safe house, but they missed the suspects by a few minutes.

→ In your groups, you will share what you know about the problem or crime and gather information from any other source that seems appropriate.

→ You will share this information among group members.

→ When you believe you have enough information, you will float possible solutions and attempt to support and debunk them until you decide on your "final" answer.

→ You will then present your answer to the larger group.

At the end of the group work, say:

→ On one flipchart, identify possible solutions to the problem.

→ On another flipchart, list what you have learned about creative problem solving, particularly tuning in to your success with clear communication, conflict resolution, critical thinking and problem solving, building trust, and using the talent of each of the people in your group.

Eco Challenges

Eco challenges increase awareness about an increasingly important issue that affects both individuals and businesses. Such challenges encourage people to commit to becoming proactive in keeping the environment cleaner and healthier. The challenges may be carried out for myriad reasons, for instance, enhancing understanding about:

- How the organization affects the environment
- What types of products or services could better take environmental needs into account
- Whether "green thinking" fits on the organization's priority list next to technology and globalization
- What organizational practices help the company to reduce its environmental impact
- Whether there is sufficient employee training on environmental protection, sustainability, and conservation
- How the organization encourages safeguarding the environment

Eco challenges aim to help participants to:

- Understand terminology (for example, green, organic, socially responsible, and alternative energy)
- Appropriately apply the term *green* to products
- Incorporate green solutions
- Integrate sustainable principles into business operations (for example, purchasing, printing, and travel)
- Raise children with habits that are commensurate with a more sustainable environment
- Evaluate customers' commitments to ecology when meeting their needs

- Stay ahead of the competition
- Collaborate with other organizations in local, regional, national, and global markets

In eco challenges, teams perform point-rated tasks within a specific time frame. After the tasks have been completed, the facilitator asks key questions about participants' experiences, obstacles, and any tasks that were new to them. Point-rated tasks might include:

- Purchasing recycled notebooks and reusable lunch containers for students in a classroom
- Setting up glass, metal, plastic, and newspaper recycle bins
- Planting a tree in a designated area
- Preparing items for shipping using appropriate-sized boxes, crumpled newspaper, and water-gummed tape
- Buying grocery items in bulk and packaging them for usage
- Distributing toxin-free hand sanitizers
- Installing a fan to supplement air conditioning and provide better circulation
- Researching clean and renewable energy sources
- Determining 10 locations for motion sensors so as to save energy (by turning off energy-consuming devices in areas where there is no motion and therefore no need for them)
- Preparing an organic meal
- Creating reminders about settings that power down computer screens when not in use
- Researching sites that present the latest environmental legislation
- Delivering reusable water bottles to community organizations
- Creating a work of art from paint chips

Perfect Phrases for Eco Challenges

Leaders might say:

→ We have committed to becoming more ecologically conscious and green in the ways in which we do business.

→ You have been divided into departmental teams (representing sales, production, management, and so on), and you will evaluate your operations to determine how you might become more green.

→ You may also decide to participate in green activities, either as a team or as individuals.

→ You will set short-term and long-term manageable goals for becoming greener.

→ We have provided a list of "green" activities with points attached that you might choose from. However, do not limit yourselves to our list—feel free to add your own creative ideas to the list, and to propose points for any additions.

→ You will be given a couple of hours this afternoon or tomorrow to carry out a green activity.

→ You will present your decisions to the larger group, and you will be judged on the basis of the "green potential" (greatest good) of your proposal and of the activity you carried out, the creativity and interest of your proposal, and the feasibility of your proposal.

Other Challenges

Other challenges include the following and may be carried out in a similar fashion to those just discussed:

Culinary challenges ask teams to compete in creating international cuisine, an Iron Chef–like competition, and/or a healthy food cook-off for the purpose of learning and practicing delegation based on individuals' skill sets, cooperation, and time management. The cooking task becomes a metaphor for how the team works together on the job.

Olympic challenges combine athletic endeavors with intelligence and concentration in order to allow teams to demonstrate teamwork and develop partnerships and results-oriented outcomes within an athletically competitive environment. The athletic endeavor becomes a metaphor for how the team works together on the job.

Tactical challenges include building and construction projects and mental tasks that combine convergent and divergent thinking. These challenges require teamwork and have relevance for companies that actually make things (such as dolls, toys, or puzzles). In some cases, groups may make the items and then donate them to charitable organizations (for example, toys to Toys for Tots or various other organizations during holiday times).

GPS hunt challenges are high-tech searches or scavenger hunts in which teams look for hidden items based on a series of clues. In addition to teamwork, groups are scored on their time management, efficiency, and collaboration as a team.

Artistic challenges might include magic, painting, song writing, and clothing design tasks that aim to develop collaboration, to get participants outside of their comfort zone, and to create a willingness to learn something new.

Expedition challenges ask participants to follow a series of routes leading to a final destination. In the process, teams have to overcome obstacles and make their way around detours, all of which require demonstrating resourcefulness, meeting and overcoming personal challenges, time management, risk taking, communication and leadership skills, and collaboration.

Intergenerational challenges ask people from several generations (traditionalists, baby boomers, gen X, and gen Y) to participate together in problem solving in order to understand and value the differing cultures and perceptions of these generations.

Goodwill challenges ask teams to compete in accumulating points for acts of kindness, acquiring donations, and selling fund-raising products. In the process, teams build morale and fondly remember shared and important experiences.

Game show challenges test teams' knowledge of their company and their competitors' companies (for example, their products, business strategies, and communication tools).

Futurist challenges inspire product or service innovation by asking teams to answer questions like:

- ❑ "What would our company press release read like in the year 2025?"
- ❑ "What will be the dropout rate in our high school system in the year 2020?"
- ❑ "What occupation will be most greatly needed in the year 2030?"
- ❑ "What will our organization look like in the year 2015?"

CHAPTER 7

Celebrating Success

I am persuaded that by now you will have experienced the joy of being creative: the inspiration, the sense of fulfillment, and the opportunity to work from your "center," to be "in the flow" more frequently, and to build on the energy of a group of people who care about the same things that you do. I am sure that as you have read through this book, asked yourself its questions, and said its perfect phrases to yourself, you will have experienced the joy at work that comes from allowing your creativity to flow freely, and from creating more and better ideas and products. And so, given the research that indicates that extrinsic reinforcement hampers creativity, one might ask at this point whether creativity isn't celebration enough in and of itself. If we put the effort in on the front end to become more creative, to build physical and emotional spaces for creativity, and to live out all of our creative potential, won't we be simply *living* in celebration, rather than having to *plan* celebrations?

But we are a communal people, and we have our pride, after all! We like to be recognized. We want to have our colleagues and families join us in our pride and joy and inspiration and in celebrating the results of time well spent, sometimes years, in the creative effort. And so, this chapter offers perfect phrases for celebrating success in the moment, at key points in the process, and at the end of a successful creative or innovative process.

Celebrating in the Moment

Celebrating in the moment is about being positive and expecting the best from ourselves and from our team. It is about appreciating others: appreciating what they contribute, appreciating who they are, and appreciating the small steps that they take every day. After all, workplace projects often take a long time to finish. We need something to boost our enthusiasm along the way! Have you ever been around people who truly appreciate you and express it enthusiastically? It's pretty nice, isn't it? It creates an atmosphere in which we feel more motivated to do our best, one in which our best has a chance to flourish and shine.

Perfect Phrases for Celebrating in the Moment

The following perfect phrases offer leaders and supervisors the words to express that moment-by-moment appreciation:

→ Great idea!
→ I like that one!
→ That really builds on Jeremy's idea!
→ Good job!
→ You rock!
→ You get the prize!
→ I so appreciate what you bring to the table.
→ Yes! We are making progress.

- → I like this direction.
- → Come to the front of the class.
- → Put your idea up on the board.
- → We're taking a snack break to celebrate a great completion of this step.
- → This team wins!
- → You all are really on track!
- → I am loving these ideas!
- → Yes!
- → We are getting there!
- → That's it.
- → This is real progress.
- → Your hard work is paying off.
- → This is right on track.
- → Let's put a star next to that idea.
- → I am framing this idea.
- → Let's keep going in this direction.
- → I think we're on to something.
- → It's getting better and better.
- → This is helpful.

In addition to expressing appreciation verbally to celebrate the small steps, managers and supervisors might increase the "fun quotient" with little prizes. For instance, they might:

- → Toss candy (jelly beans or chocolate kisses) to those who have good ideas.
- → Give Monopoly money for the best ideas.
- → Put stickers next to people's names each time they come up with a good idea.
- → Pass out paper stars for each good idea.

→ Give team members the opportunity to trade in their goodies for a larger prize, or give a larger prize to the person who has the most goodies at the end of the creativity meeting (for example, a dinner out with the boss, a day off, or a "slave" for the day).

Rewarding Creative Work

At key points on a project, inertia can set in, and team members can use a "pick-me-up." And, even if projects or solutions have not been completed, teams may have met significant objectives or accomplished substantial tasks. At these points, leaders and managers might lead the team in celebrating its accomplishments or works of particular creativity.

Perfect Prizes for Rewarding Creative Work

For instance, the boss might say:

→ Kara came up with a terrific idea this week. I want us to show her our appreciation! [Applause.] And I am funding her idea.

→ Roberto gets a certificate of appreciation for leading us so well in generating ideas yesterday. I have confidence that we will be able to craft a terrific solution from those ideas.

→ I'm ordering drinks (or chocolate cake) for everyone. We have done a terrific job at generating ideas at this stage of the project.

→ We have made such substantial progress in such a great direction that I'm taking everyone out to dinner.

→ You've done great work today. You can come in late tomor-row [or sleep in, or take some time off].

→ Saralee's idea generated so much excitement in the board of directors' meeting that she has earned herself a spa day.

→ The execs thought our ideas were so outstanding that they have given you each a small bonus.

→ Our last creativity meeting was so successful that the vice president has funded us to hold our next one at the Boulder Retreat Center—as you know, it has great food, great hiking areas, a spa, and meeting rooms with great views.

→ Michaela earned herself a promotion with her idea last week. I wonder how many other promotions will come out of our work on this initiative?

Perfect Phrases for Recognizing Accomplishments

And when the task is completed, the problem solved, and the creative ideas generated or actualized, then celebration is truly earned. Any of the prizes in the last section may be appropriate, and the following perfect phrases start the celebration and give credit where credit is due:

→ Stellar work!
→ A really great job!
→ We are very proud of you and your accomplishments.
→ We value you and the ideas you have.
→ You stand head and shoulders above the rest.
→ Your ideas speak for themselves.
→ Sometimes a star comes along.

➜ Your hard work has really paid off.
➜ You deserve all the praise you get.
➜ We are happy to have you working for us.
➜ Your work stands out and deserves recognition.
➜ Your creativity really shines.
➜ We need more people like you working for us.
➜ You really stimulate us all to do our best.
➜ You succeeded in pulling everyone together.
➜ You are the quiet voice that triggers the best ideas.
➜ I am proud to have hired you.
➜ I am happy to work with you.
➜ You are a shining star.
➜ You should feel proud of yourself.
➜ You have accomplished much.
➜ You will go far.
➜ You have brought pride to our company.
➜ You have led your group well.
➜ Your energy has infused us all.
➜ Your ideas have energized the group.
➜ We are proud of you and your work.
➜ You are the heart and soul of our group.
➜ Your team really pulled together.
➜ This team is leading the way toward a better future.
➜ We can all now build on your team's ideas.
➜ You are all so much more than cogs in a wheel.
➜ What great energy I am experiencing as I work with you all.
➜ These ideas will take us far.
➜ You are leaving a great legacy that will have widespread positive impact.
➜ These results are far beyond our expectations.

- The energy in this team is inspiring.
- You all worked together with great results.
- We all need to tap into the creative energy you have demonstrated.
- Here's a small token of my appreciation [for example, a Starbucks card, a gift card, or a night out at a special restaurant].

CHAPTER 8

Companies and Individuals That Intentionally Tap In to Creativity

ast Company, the magazine, publishes a list of the year's "Most Innovative Companies" regularly. Following are some of the companies on their lists and what their leaders and employees had to say to *Fast Company* about their creativity and the reasons for their success.

Google

Principles

- Boundless freedom.
- Perfect perks.
- A culture that prizes spectacular failure more than middling success.
- A difference in the spirit of the place.
- Belief that their work can change the world.
- Ability to instill a sense of creative fearlessness and ambition.

- Seeing information as a natural resource, one that should be mined, refined, sorted, and universally distributed.
- The resources and liberty that Google entrusts to its workers infuse them with a rare sense of possibility—and obligation.

Perfect Phrases from Employees

Prospective hires were asked, "If you could change the world using Google's resources, what would you build?"

"I'm . . . fascinated by tools that make it easier for people to explore their worlds."
                              —Douglas Merrill, CIO and VP of engineering

About culture: "Google lives it out loud. We argue about everything. But you want conflict to thrive in a supportive way."
                              —Marissa Mayer

"We let engineers spend 20 percent of their time working on whatever they want, and we trust that they'll build interesting things."
                              —Marissa Mayer

"But research isn't off in a corner here. It happens everywhere, because everybody does research."
                              —T. V. Raman

"User stories went into a database that we shared with other teams. That's how we cross the silos."

—Irene Au

"We try to out-innovate each other. We built the tools and infrastructure to leverage the outside developer community."

—Jessica Ewing

"Even if you don't always achieve 100 percent of audacious goals, you're probably doing better than if you set milder goals."

—Bill Weihl

"The attitude is to pursue ideas that another company dismisses as outside the realm of possibility."

—Niniane Wang

"Google has a high tolerance for chaos and ambiguity. When in doubt, do something. If you have two paths and you're not sure which is right, take the fastest path."

—David Glazer

"Wow, you hire a guy who's an expert in food and let him run with it! You don't get in his way or micromanage."

—Josef Desimone

"Commonsense stuff. There are not a lot of rules and regulations."

—Andy Rubin

"At Google, there are rocks and a stream. You either become a rock, and the stream goes around you, or you get in the stream and move things along and start adding value. People here don't start with conclusions. They start with questions."

—Tim Armstrong

"We also have the resources of talented and socially engaged Googlers. That's our greatest asset. We began with thousands of ideas from Googlers and others in the field and winnowed them down."

—Larry Brilliant

Apple

Principles

- Orchestrate and integrate. Ideas can come from anywhere, including outside the company.
- Trust your instinct. Don't allow the customer to dictate what you do.
- There's no success like failure. Fail often, fail fast, and fail well. In other words, don't be afraid to make a mistake, but always learn from your mistakes.
- Safe is risky. Develop products that define new categories and markets rather than products that compete in existing markets.
- Seduce customers.
- Make a great product that people want to have and they will be willing to pay more for it. On top of that, they will also help you sell it to all their friends and colleagues.

- Empathy with the user is a powerful tool for innovation. It gives you insight into the problem and makes you care about the outcome.
- Put resources behind a few products and commit to making those products exceptionally well.
- Subtraction often adds value.

Perfect Phrases from Steve Jobs, Former CEO

→ "It's like when I walk into a room and I want to talk about a product that hasn't been invented yet. I can see the product as if it's sitting there right in the center of the table. It's like what I've got to do is materialize it and bring it to life."

→ "These products have always existed; it's just that no one had ever seen them before. We were the ones who discovered them."

→ "We tend to focus much more. Focus means saying no to the hundred other good ideas that there are. You have to pick carefully."

→ "We have a short period of time on this earth. . . . My feeling is that I've got to accomplish a lot of things while I'm young."

→ "Get rid of the crappy stuff."

Facebook

Principles

- Love of risk.
- Boot camp—a six-week cultural indoctrination into the company's code and customs for incoming engineers. Words that one hears constantly are fight, entrepreneurial, and impact.
- Hacking, described as a mix of arrogance and curiosity.
- The importance of rapid deployment and iteration.
- "Hackathons," all-hands, all-night meetings raised to an art form, held every other month or so. The company provides food, music, and beer.

Perfect Phrases from Employees

"We move very fast. And we definitely fight. We expect people to be passionate, and they're going to fight to make their case. Facebook is free-form. If you're not coming up with new ideas, then you're just along for the ride. We win our fights through prototyping. We get our ideas out there."

—Andrew "Boz" Bosworth

"If we had an idea, we could make it live right away. That's how I enjoy developing things." [About hacking]: "The root of the hacker mindset is, 'There's a better way.' Just because people have been doing it the same way since the beginning of time, I'm going to make it better.

You can push your code out daily to a group of users to test."

—Paul Buchheit

"Hacking is not about breaking and entering. It's about being unafraid to break things in order to make them better."

—Mark Zuckerberg

[Of the countless product changes that happen over the course of a week, month, and year]: "What we make won't last, but we make things fast and get to test our ideas quickly with real users. We're in it for the impact."

—Soleio Cuervo

Nissan

Nissan created the Leaf, the first mass-market, all-electric car.

Principles

- Consciousness that something has to be done
- Investing in technology
- Responding to a problem: emissions

Perfect Phrases from Carlos Ghosn, CEO

→ "We're going to make different solutions. We're not going to stubbornly defend one technology."
→ "People need to feel the passion, vision, determination, and focus."

→ "Change has always been part of my life."
→ "Spend time in an emerging market. Look at how people spend their time, what they do for fun. See how people live."
→ "Every generation needs to learn how to relearn."
→ "You're going to have to adapt to the new technology. It's not easy, but it's not impossible."

Pixar

Principles

■ Culture is defined by a pursuit of excellence and quality.
■ Find ways to fail quickly, to invest less emotion and less time in any particular idea, prototype, or piece of work.
■ A small team does everything (the story and the technology), and this allows people to stretch.
■ Everyone owns the project.
■ New movies do not begin with a script; they begin with a storyboard (27,565 storyboards for *A Bug's Life*; 43,536 for *Finding Nemo*; 69,562 for *Ratatouille*; and 98,173 for *WALL-E*).
■ Films will "suck" virtually until the last stage of production.

Perfect Phrases from Pixar

John Lasseter, Pixar's chief creative officer:

→ "We don't actually finish our films, we release them."
→ "In a hierarchy, everyone is working for the person making the film, but we push control far down into the organization."
→ "If we're not scared, really scared, we're not doing a good project."

President Ed Catmull's description of Pixar's creative process:

→ "Going from suck to nonsuck."

Andrew Stanton, director of *Finding Nemo* and *WALL-E*:

→ "My strategy has always been: be wrong as fast as we can."
→ "We're gonna screw up, let's just admit that. Let's not be afraid of that."
→ "Sometimes the first try works, while other times a dozen or more passes are required."

Zynga

Zynga is the fastest-growing game company in history. It attracts 300 million people a month to play its titles. Zynga creates social gaming, known as "casual games," or colorful alternative universes in which people raise avatar families in FrontierVille and crops in FarmVille and spend real money to buy virtual goods to fill their imaginary places.

Principles

■ Aggressively embrace lightweight and addictive social gaming.
■ Relentlessly focus on speed and data gathering.
■ Measure every aspect of the game experience with analytics, so that employees can evaluate users' behavior to improve every game every day.
■ Be thoughtful and probing, ask questions, and want to create the right culture for the company.
■ Constantly search for new ways to give employees a sense of creative ownership.
■ The leader radiates a fundamental decency.

Perfect Phrases from Mark Pincus, CEO

➜ "We're giving people a reliable 15 minutes a day that lets them not only play, but also connect with people in their lives with some level of meaning."

➜ "I've failed a lot," he says. "I've been fired a lot."

➜ "This is about building something that people can't remember life before it and can't live without."

➜ "Analytics are usually seen quarterly. I wanted it to be part of the culture."

➜ "Everyone is the CEO of the thing that they do."

➜ "We should all feel lucky to live in such a transformative time."

IDEO

Principles

■ Build on the ideas of others.

■ Share information outside of your own walls.

■ Generate ideas collectively.

■ Create a company with 360 degrees of innovation.

■ A devil's advocate is toxic to creativity; instead, have 10 others in the room:

❑ **The Anthropologist** brings new learning and insights into the organization by observing human behavior and developing a deep understanding of how people interact physically and emotionally with products, services, and spaces.

❑ **The Experimenter** prototypes new ideas continuously, learning by a process of enlightened trial and error.

❑ **The Cross-Pollinator** explores other industries and cultures, then translates those findings and revelations to fit the unique needs of your enterprise.

❑ **The Hurdler** knows that the path to innovation is strewn with obstacles and develops a knack for overcoming or outsmarting those roadblocks.

❑ **The Collaborator** helps bring eclectic groups together, and often leads from the middle of the pack to create new combinations and multidisciplinary solutions.

❑ **The Director** not only gathers together a talented cast and crew, but also helps to spark their creative talents.

❑ **The Experience Architect** designs compelling experiences that go beyond mere functionality to connect with customers' latent or expressed needs at a deeper level.

❑ **The Set Designer** creates a stage on which innovation team members can do their best work, transforming physical environments into powerful tools to influence behavior and attitudes.

❑ **The Caregiver** builds on the metaphor of a healthcare professional to deliver customer care in a manner that goes beyond mere service.

❑ **The Storyteller** builds both internal morale and external awareness through compelling narratives that communicate a fundamental human value or reinforce a specific cultural trait.

■ Follow strict rules for sparking good ideas:

❑ Sharpen the focus with a well-honed statement of the problem.

❑ Write playful rules, such as "defer judgment" and "one conversation at a time."

❑ Number your ideas to motivate people (say, "Let's shoot for 100 ideas!").

❑ Build momentum, get out of the way, and jump back in when momentum starts to fade.

❑ Make the space remember by writing ideas down on accessible surfaces (for example, easel-sized sticky notes).

❑ Stretch your mental muscles with brainstorming warm-ups.

❑ Get physical by creating and then "showing and telling."

Perfect Phrases from Tom Kelley, CEO

➜ Idea-generation exercises are "practically a religion."

➜ "When you're stuck, you have a social obligation to get help."

➜ "We have more recently come around to seeing innovation as a tool for transforming the entire culture of organizations."

➜ "Companies need innovation at every point of the compass, in all aspects of the business, and in every team member."

➜ "All good working definitions of innovation pair ideas with action, the spark with the fire. Innovators don't just have their heads in the clouds. They also have their feet on the ground."

Whole Foods

Principles

- Make food shopping a mouth-watering adventure.
- All work is teamwork.
- Everyone sees the numbers.
- The first prerequisite of effective teamwork is trust, and so there is an open-salary policy.
- People vote on who gets hired.
- Democracy with discipline.
- A strong sense of community with a fierce commitment to productivity.
- The "gain-sharing" program ties bonuses directly to team performance—specifically, sales per labor hour.

Perfect Phrases from Leaders

"I'm not the one you need to impress. It's your fellow team members."

—Ron Megahan

"Here's what I'm making; here's what [cofounder] Craig Weller is making—heck, here's what everybody's making [referring to salaries]."

—John Mackey

References

1. Adams, James L. *The Care and Feeding of Ideas: A Guide to Encouraging Creativity*. Reading, MA: Addison-Wesley, 1986.
2. Cameron, Julia. *The Artist's Way: A Spiritual Path to Higher Creativity*. New York: Penguin Putnam, 2002.
3. Cassandro, Vincent J., and Dean K. Simonton. "Creativity and Genius." In *Flourishing: Positive Psychology and the Life Well-Lived*, edited by C. L. M. Keyes and J. Haidt. Washington, DC: American Psychological Association, 2003.
4. Colligan, Victoria, Beth Schoenfeldt, and Amy Swift. *Ladies Who Launch: Embracing Entrepreneurship and Creativity as a Lifestyle*. New York: St. Martin's Press, 2007.
5. Commons, Michael, and Linda Bresette. "Major Creative Innovators as Viewed Through the Lens of the General Model of Hierarchical Complexity and Evolution." In *Creativity, Spirituality, and Transcendence: Paths to Integrity and Wisdom in the Mature Self*, edited by Melvin Miller and Susanne Cook-Greuter, pp. 151–166. Stamford, CT: Ablex Publishing, 2000.
6. Cook-Greuter, Susanne, and Melvin Miller. "Introduction: Creativity in Adulthood. In *Creativity, Spirituality, and Transcendence: Paths to Integrity and Wisdom in the Mature Self*, edited by Melvin Miller and Susanne Cook-Greuter. Stamford, CT: Ablex Publishing, 2000.

7. de Bono, Edward. *Six Thinking Hats*. Boston: Little, Brown & Company, 1985.

8. Department of Energy, Management Oversight Risk Tree (MORT) NASA, retrieved July 15, 2011, from http://en.wikipedia.org/wiki/Root_cause_analysis.

9. Foster, Jack. *How to Get Ideas*. San Francisco: Barrett Koehler, 2007.

10. Glass-Solomon, Stephanie, and Cheryl Armon. "Lifelong Learning and the Good Life: Reconceiving Adult Education for Development." In *Creativity, Spirituality, and Transcendence: Paths to Integrity and Wisdom in the Mature Self*, edited by Melvin Miller and Susanne Cook-Greuter, pp. 189–208. Stamford, CT: Ablex Publishing, 2000.

11. Goleman, Daniel, Paul Kaufman, and Michael Ray. *The Creative Spirit*. New York: Dutton, 1992.

12. Hemsley Fraser. *Assessing Opportunities*. Waltham, MA: Hemsley Fraser, 2011.

13. Hightower, Rose. *Internal Controls Policies and Procedures*. Hoboken, NJ: John Wiley & Sons, 2008, p. 83.

14. Johansson, Frans. *The Medici Effect*. Boston: Harvard Business School, 2004.

15. Johnston, Robert, and Douglas Bate. *The Power of Strategy Innovation: A New Way of Linking Creativity and Strategic Planning to Discover Great New Business Opportunities*. Washington, DC: American Management Association, 2003.

16. Kotter, John. *The Heart of Change*. Boston: Harvard Business School, 2002.

17. Mednick, S. The Associative Basis of the Creative Process. *Psychological Review*, 69(3), 1962, pp. 220–232.

18. Michalko, Michael. *Thinkertoys*. Berkeley, CA: Ten Speed Press, 2006.

19. Miller, Melvin, and Suzanne Cook-Greuter. "Edith Kramer—Artist and Art Therapist: A Search for Integrity and Truth." In *Creativity, Spirituality, and Transcendence: Paths to Integrity and Wisdom in the Mature Self,* edited by Melvin Miller and Susanne Cook-Greuter, pp. 99–124. Stamford, CT: Ablex Publishing, 2000.

20. Murray, David K. *Borrowing Brilliance.* New York: Gotham Books, 2009.

21. Ohno, Taiichi. *Toyota Production System: Beyond Large-Scale Production.* Portland, OR: Productivity Press, 1988.

22. Peterson, Christopher, and Martin Seligman. *Character Strengths and Virtues: A Handbook and Classification.* New York: Oxford, 2004.

23. Ray, Michael, and Rochelle Myers. *Creativity in Business.* New York: Doubleday, 1986.

24. Silverstein, David, Philip Samuel, and Neil DeCarlo. *The Innovator's Toolkit: 50+ Techniques for Predictable and Sustainable Organic Growth.* Hoboken, NJ: John Wiley & Sons, 2009.

25. Simonton, Dean. *Origins of Genius.* New York: Oxford, 1999.

26. Straus, Steven D. *The Big Idea: How Business Innovators Get Great Ideas to Market.* Chicago: Dearborn Trade Publishing, 2002.

27. Vamos, Mark N., David Lidsky, and Jim Collins (eds.). *Fast Company's Greatest Hits: Ten Years of the Most Innovative Ideas in Business.* New York: Penguin Group, 2004.

28. Zebrowski, Ernest. "Scientist and Artist Within the Mature Self: The Integration of Two Worlds." In *Creativity, Spirituality, and Transcendence: Paths to Integrity and Wisdom in the Mature Self,* edited by Melvin Miller and Susanne Cook-Greuter, pp. 151–166. Stamford, CT: Ablex Publishing, 2000.

About the Author

Dr. Karen Eriksen's passion has always been transforming lives so as to make a difference in the world. In her work life, this began with missionary and counseling work, transforming individual and family systems spiritually, emotionally, and behaviorally. Later, her efforts included supervising, teaching, and developing courses, programs, and training experiences that would transform group and classroom experiences for counseling students who were aiming to become expert professionals. Currently, she transforms organizations from the top down, helping leaders and managers to develop the tools necessary to stimulate change and innovation and to create healthy and fully functional organizations in which employees can work and create optimally. Her gift is triggering the energy of group processes, in which participants create solutions that are more and bigger and better than those they could create on their own. Her courses, trainings, and talks have been very well received, and she has obtained top evaluations from participants.

Karen's company, the Eriksen Institute, offers corporate training and consultation, course design, continuing education, and public speaking on topics that help organizations to operate optimally, which includes triggering systems that enable their employees to function optimally. Optimal organizations begin with deciding about centering values, and with infusing those values throughout the company. Company leaders then need the tools to act on those values, including communication and conflict-resolution skills, ethical decision-making skills, and skills in developing ethical compliance procedures. Karen also serves as a trainer and course designer for Hemsley Fraser/Booz Allen Hamilton in federal government transformation initiatives. The courses she develops and facilitates assist individuals and teams in using creative and innovative problem-solving and change-management strategies to transform organizations.

Karen is a well-published author in the academic arena, having written 9 books and an ethics and life skills curriculum, 22 peer-reviewed articles, 16 other articles, and 6 book chapters related to interpersonal skills and functioning, adult development, ethical development, spirituality, diagnosis, counselor competence, and diversity. She also developed a television talk show, "To Your Health," that quickly became a favorite on public television.

More on Karen's trainings, speeches, course and program design, and consultation is available at www.erikseninstitute.com. She can be reached through the website or at karen@erikseninstitute.com.

The Right Phrase for Every Situation…Every Time.

Perfect Phrases for Building Strong Teams
Perfect Phrases for Business Letters
Perfect Phrases for Business Proposals and Business Plans
Perfect Phrases for Business School Acceptance
Perfect Phrases for College Application Essays
Perfect Phrases for Communicating Change
Perfect Phrases for Conflict Resolution
Perfect Phrases for Cover Letters
Perfect Phrases for Creativity and Innovation
Perfect Phrases for Customer Service, 2e
Perfect Phrases for Dealing with Difficult People
Perfect Phrases for Dealing with Difficult Situations at Work
Perfect Phrases for Documenting Employee Performance Problems
Perfect Phrases for Employee Development Plans
Perfect Phrases for ESL Everyday Business
Perfect Phrases for Executive Presentations
Perfect Phrases for Fundraising
Perfect Phrases for Health Professionals
Perfect Phrases for Icebreakers
Perfect Phrases for Landlords and Property Managers
Perfect Phrases for Law School Acceptance
Perfect Phrases for Lead Generation
Perfect Phrases for Leadership Development
Perfect Phrases for Lean Six Sigma
Perfect Phrases for Letters of Recommendation
Perfect Phrases for Managers and Supervisors, 2e
Perfect Phrases for Managing Your Small Business
Perfect Phrases for Medical School Acceptance
Perfect Phrases for Meetings
Perfect Phrases for Motivating and Rewarding Employees, 2e
Perfect Phrases for Negotiating Salary & Job Offers
Perfect Phrases for New Employee Orientation and Onboarding
Perfect Phrases for Office Professionals
Perfect Phrases for Perfect Hiring
Perfect Phrases for the Perfect Interview
Perfect Phrases for Presenting Business Strategies:
Perfect Phrases for Performance Reviews, 2e
Perfect Phrases for Professional Networking
Perfect Phrases for Real Estate Agents & Brokers
Perfect Phrases for Resumes
Perfect Phrases for Sales and Marketing Copy
Perfect Phrases for the Sales Call, 2e
Perfect Phrases for Setting Performance Goals, 2e
Perfect Phrases for Six Sigma
Perfect Phrases for Managing Your Small Business
Perfect Phrases for the TOEFL Speaking and Writing Sections
Perfect Phrases for Virtual Teams
Perfect Phrases for Writing Employee Surveys
Perfect Phrases for Writing Grant Proposals
Perfect Phrases for Writing Job Descriptions
Perfect Phrases in American Sign Language for Beginners
Perfect Phrases in French for Confident Travel
Perfect Phrases in German for Confident Travel
Perfect Phrases in Italian for Confident Travel
Perfect Phrases in Spanish for Confident Travel to Mexico
Perfect Phrases in Spanish for Construction
Perfect Phrases in Spanish for Gardening and Landscaping
Perfect Phrases in Spanish for Household Maintenance and Childcare
Perfect Phrases in Spanish for Restaurant and Hotel Industries

Visit mhprofessional.com/perfectphrases for a complete product listing.

Learn more. Do more.